The Philosophy of
Agamben

Continental European Philosophy

This series provides accessible and stimulating introductions to the ideas of continental thinkers who have shaped the fundamentals of European philosophical thought. Powerful and radical, the ideas of these philosophers have often been contested, but they remain key to understanding current philosophical thinking as well as the current direction of disciplines such as political science, literary theory, social theory, art history, and cultural studies. Each book seeks to combine clarity with depth, introducing fresh insights and wider perspectives while also providing a comprehensive survey of each thinker's philosophical ideas.

Published titles

The Philosophy of Agamben
Catherine Mills

The Philosophy of Derrida
Mark Dooley and Liam Kavanagh

The Philosophy of Foucault
Todd May

The Philosophy of Gadamer
Jean Grondin

The Philosophy of Habermas
Andrew Edgar

The Philosophy of Hegel
Allen Speight

The Philosophy of Kierkegaard
George Pattison

The Philosophy of Merleau-Ponty
Eric Matthews

The Philosophy of Nietzsche
Rex Welshon

The Philosophy of Schopenhauer
Dale Jacquette

Forthcoming titles include

The Philosophy of Husserl
Burt Hopkins

The Philosophy of Kant
James O'Shea

The Philosophy of Sartre
Anthony Hatzimoysis

The Philosophy of Agamben

Catherine Mills

McGill-Queen's University Press
Montreal & Kingston • Ithaca

ISBN 978-0-7735-3487-2 (hardcover)
ISBN 978-0-7735-3488-9 (paperback)

Legal deposit fourth quarter 2008
Bibliothèque nationale du Québec

Published simultaneously outside North America by
Acumen Publishing Limited

McGill-Queen's University Press acknowledges the financial support of
the Government of Canada through the Book Publishing Development
Program (BPIDP) for its activities.

Library and Archives Canada Cataloguing in Publication
Mills, Catherine, 1972–
    The philosophy of Agamben / Catherine Mills.

(Continental European philosophy 11)
Includes bibliographical references and index.
ISBN 978-0-7735-3487-2 (bound).—ISBN 978-0-7735-3488-9 (pbk.)
    1. Agamben, Giorgio, 1942–. I. Title. II. Series.

B3611.A42M45 2008   195   C2008-903737-5

Typeset by Graphicraft Limited, Hong Kong.
Printed and bound by Biddles Limited, King's Lynn.

For Dave
(1936–1991)

Contents

Acknowledgements

After reading and discussing Agamben's work for some years, I have acquired too many debts to interlocutors to acknowledge adequately here and, for the most part, I can express my gratitude only in general terms. However, several colleagues and friends deserve special mention for their assistance, support and encouragement. I particularly thank Rosalyn Diprose, Simon Lumsden and Paul Patton for a rare kind of collegiality. I thank Penelope Deutscher for initially prompting me to write this book, and Elizabeth Wilson for timely encouragement. Ann Murphy, Niamh Stephenson and Catherine Zimmer have helped me in incalculable ways. I am, as always, immeasurably grateful to Morgan Brigg. Special thanks also go to Mick Dillon. Sadly, Paul Fletcher died during the final stages of the production of this book and I wish to acknowledge his friendship, support and intellectual generosity here.

I acknowledge the support of the Faculty of Arts and Social Sciences of the University of New South Wales, Australia, in the form of a Postdoctoral Writing Award in 2005, which assisted by providing relief from teaching duties for a semester. Parts of this work draw on previously published articles, specifically: C. Mills, "Agamben's Messianic Politics: Biopolitics, Abandonment and Happy Life", *Contretemps* 5, 2004, 42–62; C. Mills, "Playing with Law: Agamben and Derrida on Post-Juridical Justice", Alison Ross (ed.), "The Agamben Effect", *South Atlantic Quarterly* 107(1), 2007, 15–36; C. Mills, "Linguistic Survival and Ethicality: Biopolitics, Subjectivation and Testimony in *Remnants of Auschwitz*", in *Politics, Metaphysics and Death: Essays on Giorgio Agamben's Homo Sacer*. A. Norris (ed.), Durham, NC: Duke University Press, 2005, 198–221.

Abbreviations

Full bibliographical details of the works listed here are given in the Bibliography.

AI   "Absolute Immanence". In *Potentialities: Collected Essays in Philosophy*

B   "Bartleby, or on Contingency". In *Potentialities: Collected Essays in Philosophy*

CC   *The Coming Community*

EP   *The End of the Poem: Studies in Poetics*

FPI   "For a Philosophy of Infancy". In *Public* **21**
http://www.yorku.ca/public/backissu/v21_1.html

HS   *Homer Sacer: Sovereign Power and Bare Life*

IH   *Infancy and History: Essays on the Destruction of Experience*

IL   "The Idea of Language". In *Potentialities: Collected Essays in Philosophy*

IP   *Idea of Prose*

K   "Kommerell, or On Gesture". In *Potentialities: Collected Essays in Philosophy*

LD   *Language and Death: The Place of Negativity*

LH   "Language and History". In *Potentialities: Collected Essays in Philosophy*

ME   *Means without End: Notes on Politics*

MS   "The Messiah and the Sovereign: The Problem of Law in Walter Benjamin". In *Potentialities: Collected Essays in Philosophy*

MWC   *The Man Without Content*

O   *The Open: Man and Animal*

OP   "On Potentiality". In *Potentialities: Collected Essays in Philosophy*

P   *Profanations*

RA   *Remnants of Auschwitz*

S   *Stanzas: Word and Phantasm in Western Culture*
SE   *State of Exception*
TI   "The Thing Itself". In *Potentialities: Collected Essays in Philosophy*
TR   *The Time That Remains: A Commentary on the Letter to the Romans*
WIP   "What Is a Paradigm?", http://www.egs.edu/faculty/agamben/agamben-what-is-a-paradigm-2002.html
WP   "*Pardes*: The Writing of Potentiality". In *Potentialities: Collected Essays in Philosophy*

Introduction

Giorgio Agamben has become well known in recent years for his interventions in political theory, ethics and questions of law. Since the translation
of his enigmatic work, *The Coming Community*, in 1993, English publication of his work has occurred at an ever-increasing rate. In the process,
his complex and philosophically dense reflections on contemporary problems of sovereignty, biopolitics and ethics have transformed the terms of
much of the critical discourse of radical theory. Terms such as sovereignty,
the exception, biopolitics and life can scarcely be used today without reference to Agamben. Moreover, his approach to questions of language,
subjectivity and representation has reoriented discussion away from the
deconstructive approach that has largely dominated in the Anglo-American
context of late. In doing so, it has lent these questions a new philosophical
importance by recasting their status within the history of philosophy, and
especially in relation to the perceived metaphysical propensity to found
humanity on negativity alone. As such, his work has also helped to reopen
questions of philosophical anthropology, contributing to a renewed interest in the distinction between animality and humanity.

Despite the critical interventions of his work, however, the concepts
he develops and their philosophical importance remain obscure to many.
This is in no small part because of the sheer complexity and difficulty of his
work. There are several sources of this complexity, the first of which is simply its breadth of reference. In often sharp contrast to most contemporary
philosophers and theorists, Agamben is perhaps more akin to the classical
learned figure of the Italian Renaissance – schooled in various fields of
study, including aesthetics, religion, politics, law and ethics, rigorously
faithful to the original text, and studiously attentive to philological detail.
Often, a detail from a foundational but more or less forgotten cultural icon
or text will provide Agamben with the kernel of his argument, generating
and guiding a deep interpretation and intricate conceptual apparatus. For

example, his book *The Open* begins with a detail from a thirteenth-century Hebrew Bible, whereas earlier works such as *The End of the Poem* and *Stanzas* draw on classic *Stilnovo* love poetry, the drawings of Grandville and Dürer's figure of *Melancholia*.

Another source of complexity is Agamben's own stylistics. In contrast to the digressions and convolutions to which many have become accustomed through reading figures such as Martin Heidegger or, more recently, Jacques Derrida and his deconstructive followers, Agamben's style is compact to the point of ellipsis. Most of his books are short – often fewer than 150 pages – but this does not make them easy reading. Instead, highly compacted arguments and insights are presented without explication but with a sharp elegance that provokes as much as it compels. Additionally, and more importantly, over the past several decades Agamben has used various literary forms within ostensibly philosophical texts in what is ultimately a complex exercise in pushing philosophy to its limits. His arguments and thoughts are developed through fragments, interpolated "thresholds" and crystalline essays that leave little room for the extensive and patient work of setting out propositions, drawing conclusions and pre-emptively rebutting counter-claims that characterizes much philosophy.

Related to this, Agamben's *œuvre* does not develop in such a way as to allow a progressive and systematic understanding to be gained through further reading. The reader who hopes to throw further light on a claim made in one text can often find the same claim made elsewhere, sometimes with different refractions and modifications, but these do not add up to a philosophical system as such. In fact, if one reads progressively through Agamben's work, it is evident that there is very little sense in which it follows a straightforward incremental or systematic trajectory. Instead, his work over the past several decades is a complex recursive exercise that extends and modifies his approach to several key questions and issues that reappear in one guise or another in almost every text. In this way, there is a densely interconnected conceptual web, but no (more or less linear) system as such. For instance, issues raised but barely addressed in early works such as *Language and Death* form the basis of an extended reflection in later works such as *The Open*. But this does not so much complete or address an inadequacy in the earlier text as reinterpret an aspect of the problem at hand. As this suggests, then, despite their ostensible diversity, several core concerns unite Agamben's various works, ensuring an unmistakeable continuity across them.

One of these concerns, and arguably the most central one, is the question of what it means to say "I speak". Agamben himself indicates the centrality of this problem in his self-interpretation offered in the preface to the English translation of *Infancy and History*. While such self-interpretations are not always to be taken at face value, in this case it is unquestionably accurate. The question of what it means to say "I speak" crystallizes a number of threads of enquiry that run throughout Agamben's *œuvre*. The most obvious of these is the question of language itself: what is language and what is it to speak? What is it to be a being that has language? What is "I"? These questions yield several sets of problems for Agamben and, in his view, have immeasurable consequence across fields such as politics, ethics and aesthetics.

The first of these, which I discuss under the broad heading of "Metaphysics" in Chapter 1, addresses the way in which language has been thought of as a "faculty" or capacity of the human being in Western philosophy. Agamben takes this up through a discussion of Heidegger and Hegel in *Language and Death*. He argues that both these master thinkers maintain a view of language grounded in negativity, which he encapsulates in the notion of Voice. For Agamben, the grounding of language in negativity relegates human nature to emptiness or nothingness, that is, nihilism. For him, the only way beyond this is to found a new experience of the taking place of language in what he calls "infancy", which is purified of any reference to the negative ground of a silent or ineffable Voice. The notion of "infancy" does not simply refer here to a stage of human development, but instead indexes a mute experience of language that precedes speech, and that is also appropriated in speech.

Related to this is the problem of potentiality or possibility, which Agamben addresses through returning to Aristotle's discussion of it in his *Metaphysics*. Crucial to Agamben's interpretation is the emphasis he places, first, on the necessary relation between potentiality and privation, such that potentiality must always maintain a relation to impotentiality or impossibility in the passage to actuality. Secondly, though, he also stresses the suspension of the passage of potentiality into actuality, such that actuality itself appears not simply as "being" or "doing" but, rather, as "not not-being" or "not not-doing". In this, actuality appears as the negation of *im*-potentiality, or to put the point another way, the negation of negation. This formulation of potentiality and actuality underlies much of Agamben's formulation of political liberation, which I discuss in the later chapters of the book. More generally, the logic of suspension and the negation of negation prove to be important thematics throughout much of his work.

Chapter 2 extends the discussion of a new experience of language discussed in Chapter 1, and also begins to look towards the terms of analysis of Agamben's political and ethical thought. It focuses first on the distinction between poetics and philosophy, which gives rise to a notion of criticism that exceeds the models of representation and language presupposed by either side of the traditional opposition. Central to this section of the chapter is a further discussion of what Agamben calls the "thing" itself of language, or the *Idea* of language, through which he draws attention to the possibility of a pure language that communicates nothing other than its own communicability. Secondly, the chapter provides an extended discussion of Agamben's approach to the object – understood as both the object of knowledge and thus representation, and as the object of aesthetics and of consumption. In this, I outline his discussion of fetishism in *Stanzas*, and the necessity he suggests here of a relation to the object that allows for the appropriation of the inappropriable. The chapter covers the texts of *The End of the Poem*, *Stanzas*, *The Man Without Content* and several other key essays.

In Chapter 3, I turn to Agamben's more recent interventions in politics, for which he is probably best known. In this chapter, I focus most specifically on Agamben's theorization of biopolitics, particularly as he negotiates this through the theory of sovereignty posed by Carl Schmitt, and Walter Benjamin's understanding of legal violence and the exceptional nature of modern politics. In the first section of the chapter, I outline Agamben's mediation of the debate between Schmitt and Benjamin, and his ultimate resolution of this in favour of the latter. In the second part of the chapter, I focus on the notion of "bare life". Central as this concept is to Agamben's political thought and critical approach to law, it is highly ambiguous. I clarify its meaning and implications, and in doing so, contextualize Agamben in relation to contemporaries such as Antonio Negri and the French philosopher Gilles Deleuze, especially in terms of their differing approaches to potentiality, sovereignty and life. This chapter provides an overview of Agamben's contribution to and position within radical political theory today. It thereby draws out some of the implications of Agamben's approach to potentiality discussed earlier, and also provides the necessary background for the following chapters on ethics and messianism.

While Chapter 3 deals with two instalments of the Homo Sacer series, *Homo Sacer* and *State of Exception*, Chapter 4 addresses *Remnants of Auschwitz*. In this text, Agamben addresses the ethical consequences of his claim that all normative thought is currently beset by nihilism. I address Agamben's use of the camps as a paradigm of biopolitical sovereignty and the nihilism that it thrives on, and consider some of the consequences of his rejection of all forms of regulative thought. I begin by outlining his theorization of an ethics based on the idea of an "unassumable responsibility", in which responsibility is thought outside legalistic frameworks of obligation and contract. This leads into a short discussion of the consequent critique of rights and juridical notions of justice that Agamben's work generates, and for which it has been heavily criticized. Secondly, part of this theorization of ethics entails returning to Agamben's approach to questions of language and subjectivity. Following up on this, I discuss his characterization of language, and intersubjectivity or relationality in ethics, an issue that is especially pertinent given that *Remnants of Auschwitz* is directed towards contemporary debates on witnessing and testimony.

In Chapter 5, I return to the concept of bare life and its companion of "happy life", or "form-of-life". This idea of happy life is posed by Agamben as the necessary foundation of a politics that allows for some resolution of the *aporias* of modern biopolitical democracy. Thus, in focusing on this notion, the central concern of this chapter is Agamben's formulation of political liberation and, more specifically, the messianic completion of humanity that such liberation must entail in Agamben's view. This leads into a number of issues for discussion: first, it requires returning to the question of animality and language that Agamben mentions in *Language and Death* without taking up in detail. His book, *The Open*, provides an extended discussion of this and thereby ultimately presents a vision of completed humanity on "the last day". Secondly, the view of political liberation that Agamben posits requires discussion of the conception of time and history that he develops throughout his work, from early texts such as *Infancy and History*, and most thoroughly in *The Time that Remains*. Thirdly, it requires discussion of the notion of play and profanation that Agamben puts forward as the mechanism for fulfilling the law, diagnosed by him as being in force without significance in modern biopolitics. And finally, it entails an outline of the vision of a "better state" after the law that he suggests profanation and play can lead to, which I suggest is given clearest articulation in the enigmatic text *The Coming Community* and the idea of "whatever singularity" developed therein.

As this outline of the chapters suggests, three figures in Western thought have a recurring and fundamental influence on Agamben's thought: Aristotle, Martin Heidegger and Walter Benjamin. This is not to suggest that they are the only important figures in his work; they are not. One could name alongside these figures, philosophers such as Kant, Hegel, Nietzsche, Arendt, the art historian Aby Warburg, Italian literary figures and poets such as Dante and Caproni, and many more besides. But the conceptual matrix within which Agamben works is to a large extent derived from Aristotle, and his way of approaching these questions is through a complex mediation of Heidegger on the one hand and Benjamin on the other.

If there is one dictum around which Agamben's thought can be said to revolve, it is the definition of man as the animal that has language and can thus decide between the just and the unjust that Aristotle poses in his *Politics*. This thought provides a touchstone for Agamben, but not in the sense that he endorses it or sees it as unproblematic. Rather, in a manner of thinking that borrows from Heidegger, he sees it as both covering over the true *ethos* of the human and disclosing the direction of thought for recovering a more originary understanding of human nature. This is particularly evident in the thought of the very nature of the human being's *having* of language. While Heidegger's influence is palpable throughout Agamben's work, particularly in the earlier work and in so far as it guides a style of analysis, more often than not Benjamin provides Agamben with the conceptual tools for the resolution of the problems that he argues must be confronted today. That is, for the most part, Benjamin provides Agamben with the tools for the *euporic* overcoming of the *aporias* that he diagnoses as underpinning the violence of modern democracy and consumer capital.

This book has two aims, both of which shape its formulation and style. The first is to provide an introduction to Agamben's work to those who are unfamiliar with it. In this regard, I have tried to summarize clearly the logic of Agamben's arguments and approach to various questions throughout different texts. While I point to some of the complexity and ambiguity of his claims throughout, my primary concern has been to show the bare structure of the texts, what Agamben's key claims are, and how they fit into an overall argument. Of course, in doing so, I have had significantly to reduce the sheer density and breadth of his texts, both of which can be overwhelming for neophyte readers and distract from the main philosophical claims being made. I have thus risked giving the impression of a greater systematicity than there is in his work, both within texts and across them. But if I have sacrificed an appreciation of the style and experimentation, the partial progression and recursivity, of Agamben's texts for the sake of clarity and concision, I can only urge that the texts themselves be read with care. In this regard, then, I wholly concur with the sentiment that a book such as this cannot replace reading the works themselves, but it can nevertheless provide a guide for reading them, and this is the spirit in which I have progressed.

The second, and secondary, aim is to provide a critical interpretation of Agamben's thought. No introductory text can be written that does not in some way shape the interpretation and perhaps reception of the works it introduces. The process of selection and reduction required for the first aim means that any interpretation can only be partial and, in some sense, motivated by the author's own interests. In this case, I have for the most part attempted to maintain a fidelity to the text without assessing it from an external point of view. Nevertheless, some questions must be raised about Agamben's formulations – and indeed, many have in the critical literature that has emerged around his work. As is largely to be expected, this literature has focused on his political thought, and it is to this that I direct my own critical claims. There are deep and important questions to be asked about a political theory that looks beyond all conceptions of identity and difference, the state – including notions of rights and justice – and human life as it is currently understood towards a messianic fulfilment of history and humanity as its guiding principle. In the Conclusion I merely indicate some directions in which those questions might be taken, but I firmly believe that Agamben's work requires perspicacious, non-dogmatic and critical analysis before his version of political liberation and radicalism can be accepted.

CHAPTER ONE

Metaphysics: negativity, potentiality and death

Some of the most intractable problems that Agamben addresses in his work derive from his engagement with the history of metaphysics in Western philosophy, and particularly the tendency that he diagnoses in metaphysical thought to presuppose and posit a foundation for being and language in negativity. This position is elaborated most explicitly in the complex text, *Language and Death*, where Agamben sets himself the project of surpassing this metaphysical tendency towards negative foundation, which he argues first requires an examination of the true meaning of the terms "*Da*" and "*Diese*" central to the thought of the German philosophers Martin Heidegger and G. W. F. Hegel respectively. Throughout this book, he pursues the logic of negative foundation as it appears throughout Western metaphysical thought, particularly in the figurations of language as constituted by or founded in the ineffable or unspeakable. The task of surpassing metaphysics leads Agamben to posit the necessity of an experiment in language, in which what is at stake in language is not the ineffable that must necessarily be suppressed in speech, but the very event of language itself, the taking place of language prior to signification and meaning.

But the engagement with Heidegger and Hegel in *Language and Death* not only provides an important philosophical counterpoint to Agamben's theory of language; it also ties in with his reflections on the question of potentiality and actuality taken from Aristotle. In this chapter I show how Agamben's retheorization of the relation of potentiality and actuality is a necessary counterpart to the attempt to surpass metaphysics. Ultimately, in Agamben's view it is only through rethinking the relation of potentiality and actuality that the negative foundation of language and being that metaphysical thought repetitively posits can be brought to light – and also overcome.

While these are some of the most difficult problems addressed in Agamben's work, they are also the most central to it. As I begin to show in this chapter, the task of surpassing metaphysics – which encompasses the *experimentum linguae* that Agamben proposes, as well as the necessity of rethinking potentiality – provides a crucial conceptual basis for his contributions to politics and ethics. Thus it is only within the context of this project that these later contributions can be properly understood and assessed. A more complete discussion of these contributions will be undertaken in later chapters. The task of this chapter is simply to set out Agamben's approach to the conceptual problems of language, negativity and potentiality as a starting point for a deeper analysis in later chapters. I discuss his arguments in *Language and Death* about the metaphysical tendency to posit a negative foundation for language and being, and relate this to other conceptual problems that he addresses in works such as *Infancy and History* and *Potentialities*. This will lead to a discussion of the idea of an *experimentum linguae* in which what is at stake is language itself – encapsulated in the idea of infancy – as well as of Agamben's use of literary figures such as Melville's Bartleby, to elaborate a revised conception of the relation of actuality and potentiality. In the following chapters, I go on to explore the various consequences of Agamben's approach to these issues in the fields of aesthetics, politics and ethics.

A "methodological" point should be made about this chapter: throughout, I attempt to reconstruct the philosophical argument that Agamben makes in *Language and Death*, *Infancy and History* and other essays, and I do so without fully explaining the implications of his argument or considering its potential weaknesses. Because these texts and the problems they engage are crucial to understanding Agamben's *œuvre* and recur throughout it, setting up many of the problems that he continues to return to right up until his most recent work, I want here only to establish some of the central terms and theoretical turns of his work. We shall have more opportunity to return to his interpretations and their implications, as well as to his critical comments on various other thinkers, throughout the following chapters. Unfortunately, this makes the chapter somewhat difficult in its own right: it is extensive in terms of the material it covers (without being in the least exhaustive of Agamben's own treatment of the issues and sources) as well as somewhat compacted in its treatment of various concepts. But with this broad outline in place, it is possible to provide a more accessible and more coherent picture of various aspects of Agamben's thought in the following chapters.

Voice: the negative ground of language

[O]ur seminar sets out from the definitive cancellation of the Voice; or rather, it conceives of the Voice as never having been, and it no longer thinks the Voice, the unspeakable tradition. Its place is the *ethos*, the infantile dwelling – that is to say, without will or Voice – of man in language.   (*LD*: 104)

Published in Italian in 1982 and in English in 1991, *Language and Death* is the most extended discussion of his approach to metaphysics that Agamben provides, and is a crucial text for understanding the motivations and central concerns of his *œuvre*. Structured to reflect the development of ideas in a seminar in which Agamben participated in 1979 and 1980, the text takes as its starting point a comment made by Heidegger that "the essential relation between death and language flashes up before us, but remains still unthought" and proposes to investigate the relation noted here, thereby approaching the "crucial outer limit" of Heidegger's thought (*LD*: xi). The central questions that Agamben addresses in the text, which takes him beyond Heidegger in some respects, concern the attribution to human beings of the corresponding "faculties" for language and for death. Agamben wishes to question not only the supposed relation between language and death, but, more importantly, the supposition that these are essential faculties of the human. In his view, to do this requires an investigation of the "place [*topos*] of negativity" (*ibid*.: xi–xii).

To briefly summarize the argument of *Language and Death*, Agamben proposes that a reflection on the relation of language and death is necessarily a reflection on the place of negativity within metaphysical thought. It requires examining the Western philosophical presupposition that man is a being with the "faculties" for language and death – raising the question of whether the determination of man as speaking, mortal being does not in fact suppress rather than reveal humanity's proper nature. This determination of man as mortal, speaking being entails that the "proper dwelling place" or *ethos* of humanity is thoroughly permeated by negativity or nothingness. A reformulation of the metaphysical ungroundedness of humanity that this indicates must lead, Agamben argues, to a reflection on the problem of "Voice" as the "fundamental metaphysical problem" and "originary structure of negativity". Further, the reflection on Voice as the place of negativity leads to the insight that ethics – understood in the sense of *ethos* or proper dwelling place – must be released from the "informulability" to which metaphysics has condemned it. While the contemporary collapse of metaphysics into ethics that the grounding of humanity in negativity generates is increasingly evident as nihilism, contemporary thought has yet to escape from or go beyond this condition. The task that Agamben sets for contemporary thought, then, is to understand and ultimately redefine the nihilism that increasingly appears at the heart of humanity's ungroundedness. This, he ultimately argues, must be done through a thinking of the experience of language in which language is no longer grounded in the essential negativity of Voice.

This outline gives us but the barest skeleton of Agamben's project in *Language and Death* and related texts, and it is necessary to investigate the terms of his analysis much more closely if the problem he diagnoses in Western thought and the solution he wants to elaborate for it is to be understood. To do this, I begin with an outline of Agamben's relation to the thought of Heidegger. Often considered to be the greatest German philosopher of the twentieth century – and certainly one of the most controversial – Heidegger has an abiding influence upon Agamben's thought, although the latter's relation to the German is not without complication. The complexity of Agamben's engagement with Heidegger's thought is well evidenced in *Language and Death*. Perhaps one of the best-known elements of Heidegger's *Being and Time* is his analysis of "being-toward-death" as the own-most possibility of *Dasein*. In this, Heidegger attempts to develop an "existential" analysis (in the sense that he gives it of relating to the ontological characteristics of *Dasein* rather than to ontic or everyday understandings) of death, in which he argues that death is the "own-most possibility" of *Dasein*. In spite of the veiling of death in everyday understandings, for *Dasein* in an authentic relation to death, dying is revealed as a non-relational, radically individualizing possibility because of its unavoidability and intrinsicality in life – not in the sense of an event that is yet to come or as some aspect of life that is "outstanding" and yet to be incorporated into the whole, but as the condition of existential being.

Commenting on this understanding of death, Agamben emphasizes that Heidegger's characterization of *Dasein* entails that it is entirely dominated and permeated by negativity. He writes that, "together with the purely negative structure of the anticipation of death, Dasein's experience of its own-most authentic possibility coincides with its experience of the most extreme negativity" (*LD*: 2). The question that arises, then, is what the source of this negativity is – from where does the negativity that permeates *Dasein* derive? To answer this question, Agamben elucidates the "precise meaning" of the term *Dasein*, insisting that this term should be understood to mean "Being-the-*there*". It is, he suggests, exactly this formulation of *Dasein* that reveals the ontological source of negativity, since this shows that the term "*Da*" itself introduces negativity into the human, in so far as the human or *Dasein* is the being that is at home or dwells in the place of death, understood as its most authentic possibility. Thus he concludes, "negativity reaches *Dasein* from its very *Da*" (*ibid.*: 5), from its Being-the-there. Even so, this does not fully answer the question of what the source of negativity in *Dasein* is, since it says nothing about the particular power of *Da* to introduce negativity into being. Moreover, it leaves unaddressed the issue of whether the negativity that Heidegger posits as the own-most authentic possibility of *Dasein* differs from, or merely reiterates, the formulation of negativity that permeates the history of modern philosophy (*ibid.*: 4–5).

To begin to respond to these questions, Agamben turns to a discussion of negativity in the philosophy of Hegel, beginning with the observation that in Hegel's masterwork, *Phenomenology of Spirit*, the source of negativity is the demonstrative pronoun *diese*, or "this". This raises the possibility of an analogy between the Hegelian *Diese* and Heideggerian *Da*, in so far as both construe negativity as originary. Exploring this further, Agamben takes up the theme of the ineffable in Hegel's thought, the importance of which he argues is indicated by the reference to the Eleusinian mystery in the first chapter of *Phenomenology of Spirit*, which recalls an early poem by Hegel, dedicated to his friend Hölderlin in 1796. The Eleusinian mystery was an Ancient Greek cult with initiation rites revolving around Demeter (Ceres in Roman mythology), the goddess of life, agriculture and fertility, and her daughter Persephone, who, according to myth, was abducted by Hades and only permitted to emerge from the Underworld each spring. The significance of these cults here is the strict silence enforced upon initiates, who were forbidden to speak of the rites of the cult and the revelations achieved therein. Thus, in his early poem, Hegel writes of the prohibition on speech such that speech appears as a sin, as well as of the "poverty of words" and necessity of cultivating knowledge in the "breast's inner chambers" (*LD*: 9).

While the ineffable is thus guarded by silence in this poem, in the later reference in the *Phenomenology*, Hegel appears to resolve the question of the relation of the ineffable to language somewhat differently, suggesting that it is not silence that guards it, but language itself. Hegel's discussion of sense-certainty in the first chapter of the *Phenomenology* posits that utterances of "this" and "now" necessarily fail to express the meaning that the speaker wants to express, since they do not indicate the sensuous object to which they refer, but instead indicate only the universal. Thus language inadvertently expresses the true content of sense-perception while necessarily failing to say what is meant. As Hegel writes, in language "we directly refute what we mean to say, and since the universal is the true [content] of sense-certainty and language expresses this true [content] alone, it is just not possible for us ever to say, or express in words, a sensuous being that we mean."[1] Agamben emphasizes that this makes evident for Hegel the dialectic of sense-certainty, which necessarily contains negation within itself, such that "now" or "this" is always superseded by its negative and so on.

This formulation of the necessary indication of the universal and negative within language leads to Hegel's reference to the Eleusinian mysteries in the *Phenomenology*, which Agamben interprets to mean that the unspeakable is harboured within language itself. Here, the unspeakable is nothing other than meaning, the intended reference to a sensuous object that is inevitably obscured in speaking. That is, "that which is unspeakable, for language, . . . is nothing other than the very meaning, the *Meinung*, which, as such, remains necessarily unsaid in every saying: but this un-said, in itself, is simply a negative and a universal" (*LD*: 13). It is important to recognize here that the mystery of the universal is thus not harboured and protected by silence through a prohibition on speaking, but is instead cast as an unspeakable element internal to language and speaking itself. As Agamben writes, "language has captured in itself the power of silence, and that which appeared earlier as unspeakable 'profundity' can be guarded (in its negative capacity) in the very heart of the word" (*ibid.*: 13–14). Thus "all speech speaks the ineffable" (*ibid.*: 14) and demonstrates its essential characteristic as the negative or Nothingness of meaning.

Before saying more about the analogy that Agamben has thus begun to set up between Heidegger and Hegel, it is worth noting that the reference to the Eleusinian mysteries in the *Phenomenology* presages Agamben's later discussion of animality, language and world-disclosure in his book *The Open*. In this reference, Hegel suggests that animals are not excluded from the wisdom of the mysteries, but are instead "most profoundly initiated into it". This is because, rather than "standing idly in front of things . . . despairing of their reality, and completely assured of their nothingness", animals unceremoniously fall to eating them.[2] Agamben will return to this characterization of the animal's relation to the world at several points, particularly in dialogue with Heidegger's discussion of the same relation in *The Fundamental Concepts of Metaphysics*. I shall come back to this issue in due course, but for now I continue with the discussion of the metaphysical grounding of language in negativity.

So far, then, we have seen that Agamben interprets both Heidegger and Hegel as positing negativity as intrinsic to language, a point made evident in their respective characterizations of *Da* and *Diese*. For Agamben, the perceived coincidence of *Da* and *Diese* in relation to negativity raises the question of whether there is a "common essence" in these concepts that has yet to be disclosed. Noting that *Da* and *Diese* are etymologically and morphologically connected in their Greek root "*to*", he focuses on their shared grammatical status as pronouns and consequent centrality to the linguistic practice of *deixis* or indication. In the wake of the modern philosophical programme of elucidating the nature of "I" as speaking, conscious subject, modern linguistics specifies the role of the pronoun further as indicating nothing other than the taking place of utterance itself. Pronouns such as "I" and "you" – along with adverbs and other adverbial locutions such as "here", "now" and "this" – do not indicate or refer to objects outside of themselves, but instead make evident the very taking place of language itself.

That is, the use of the pronoun "I" does not refer to a psychological subject independent of language, but can refer only to the speaker of an utterance in the instance of that utterance – as Émile Benveniste writes, " 'I' signifies 'the person who utters the present instance of discourse containing "I" ' ".[3] For Benveniste, it is only in recognition of the role and function of "I" that *deixis* can be properly understood, since it reveals that "*deixis* is contemporaneous with the instance of discourse that bears the indication of the person . . . the essential thing is the relation between the indicator (of a person, a place, a time, a demonstrated object, etc.) and the *present* instance of discourse".[4] Agamben finds a parallel formulation of the role of pronouns in Roman Jakobson's explication of "shifters", or grammatical units found in code that cannot be defined outside of the message of that code. That is, they do not derive meaning from a referential relation to an object outside language, but instead operate to indicate the event of discourse itself. As Agamben writes, "the articulation – the shifting – that they effect is not from the non-linguistic (tangible indication) to the linguistic, but from *langue* to *parole*" (*LD*: 25). This shows that the proper meaning of pronouns is inseparable from the taking place of speech, such that "indication is the category within which language refers to its own taking place" (*ibid.*).

The significance of this formulation of the role of pronouns within Agamben's conceptual framework cannot be overstated. It provides him with the means of breaking with psychologistic formulations of subjectivity and, as such, is a crucial vector for his account of ethics as bearing witness to the unspeakable in speech developed in *Remnants of Auschwitz* and elsewhere. It marks his distance from attempts to posit and explain a substantive consciousness behind language and speech, which thus grounds speech as a mode of expression and communication between knowing subjects. It also proves to be a central element in the attempt to understand and move beyond the metaphysical nihilism of Western philosophy. This is because, according to Agamben, while linguistics defines this dimension as the putting into action of language through the shift from *langue* to *parole*, for more than two millennia, Western philosophy has defined it as being, or *ousia*.

For philosophy, what is indicated in the event of speech is being: thus "the dimension of meaning of the word 'being', whose eternal quest and eternal loss . . . constitute the history of metaphysics, coincides with the taking place of language . . . Only because language permits a reference to its own instance through *shifters*, something like being and the world are open to speculation" (*LD*: 25–6). This then indicates the importance of Heidegger's insight into the ontological condition of being that he claims is forgotten or covered over in the history of metaphysics, for now it appears that the ontological dimension of being "corresponds to the pure taking place of language as an originary event", and the ontic dimension of being "corresponds to that which is said and signified"; "the transcendence of being with respect to the entity, of the world with respect to the thing, is above all, a transcendence of the event of *langue* with respect to *parole*" (*ibid.*: 26). Several brief points should be noted about this claim of the relation between the transcendence of being and of language with regard to the entity and discourse respectively.

First, the formulation of this claim betrays a conceptual slippage that appears frequently throughout Agamben's work, from positing a relation of "correspondence" to positing one of identity. That is, the first formulation of the relation between the transcendence of being and language states that they "correspond", suggesting a relation of similarity or analogy, whereby one pole of the relation (e.g. being) answers to in function or character or communicates with the other (e.g. language). Importantly though, there remain two distinct poles within a relation of correspondence: the transcendence of being *and* the transcendence of language. In the second formulation, the relation posited is one of identity, whereby the transcendence of being "*is*" the transcendence of language. Certainly, it is possible to question the legitimacy of this slippage. But what is also important to say here is that it should not be thought that the identification suggested in the use of the indicative of the verb form "to be" is at all either apparent or trite. Rather, the very nature of what it is "to be" requires examination.

Secondly, then, at this point some of the complexity of Agamben's relation to Heidegger begins to become apparent, for positing a relation between the transcendence of being and language suggests congruence in their ideas concerning the history of metaphysics and the role of language within it. That is certainly the case, but there is also divergence: what motivates much of the rest of *Language and Death* is the diagnosis that both Heidegger and Hegel ultimately maintain a split or scission within language – which Agamben sees as a consistent element of Western thought from Aristotle to Wittgenstein (*LD*: 85) – in their reliance on the notion of a silent voice that acts as the "supreme shifter" between language and discourse, a voice that is itself unspeakable but that is nevertheless the condition of human discourse. Let me trace the argument that leads to this diagnosis more carefully.

If *Da* and *Diese* ought to be considered as shifters in the manner that Agamben has suggested so far, then their function is to indicate the instance of utterance, the taking place of language. Thus, for both Heidegger and Hegel, "negativity enters into man because man has to be this taking place, he wants to seize the event of language" (*LD*: 31). This raises the questions of what in this seizing of the event of language throws man into negativity and, moreover, what does it mean to indicate the taking place of language? In other words, what is the significance of construing language as something to be indicated, and what is it that allows language to show its own taking place? For Agamben, the answer to this question is "the voice", understood not simply as the medium of expression of pre- or non-verbal content, but as a "fundamental ontological dimension" to the extent that voice is presupposed in every instance of discourse. The "voice" is not simply "the mere sonorous flux emitted by the phonic apparatus" but instead incorporates being as an "unveiling and demonstration" of the event of language. This means that while the voice as sonorous flux might well index the individual animal who emits it, it cannot indicate the instance of discourse as such, and nor can it constitute an opening to the sphere of utterance and meaning. Instead, the voice as sound – or the animal *phoné* – may well be presupposed as a condition of utterance, but it is one that is *removed* in the instance of discourse as a meaning-producing activity. This opens a gap in the instance of discourse between a voice that is removed and the event of meaning, and it is in this gap that the voice appears in its ontological dimension as the revelation of being and constitutes the originary articulation or *arthron* of human language. To distinguish the ontological dimension of voice from the (ontic) voice as sound, Agamben subsequently capitalizes the term as "Voice", thereby replicating Heidegger's distinction between ontological "Being" and ontic "being".

Significantly, for Agamben, Voice is necessarily a negative articulation in so far as it has the status of a "no-longer" voice and a "not-yet" meaning: its interstitial status between the animal *phoné* and signification ensures that it is the negative ground of man's appearance in language, of his ontological grasping of the taking place of language. He writes that "[t]he Voice, as the supreme shifter that allows us to grasp the taking place of language, appears thus as the negative ground on which all ontology rests, the originary negativity sustaining every negation. For this reason, the disclosure of the dimension of being is always already threatened by nullity" (*LD*: 36). It is this construal of Voice that haunts the work of Hegel and Heidegger, and ensures that they remain within a tradition of metaphysics that rests on the articulation of negative foundation. As Agamben concludes, " *'Taking-the-*this' *and 'Being-the-*there' *are possible only through the experience of the Voice, that is, the experience of the taking place of language in the removal*

17

of the voice" (*ibid.*: 37, italics in original). The task that Agamben has ahead of him at this point is to show that such a negative articulation can indeed be found in both Hegel and Heidegger – that is, to show that each presupposes Voice as negative foundation.

In a highly compacted discussion of manuscripts from lectures presented by Hegel in Jena in 1803–4 and 1805–6, and the dialectic of "lordship and bondage" found in *Phenomenology of Spirit*, Agamben argues that the "*mythogeme*" of Voice is made apparent in Hegel's differentiation of animal voice from and transformation into human language that motivates his analysis of consciousness. Of the Jena manuscripts, Agamben focuses on the characterization of animal voice as harbouring death within itself in the claim that "every animal finds a voice in violent death, it expresses itself as a removed self (*als aufgehobnes Selbst*)" (*LD*: 45), to claim that it is by virtue of the fact that animal voice is not wholly empty – without meaning or determinate significance – that it can become the voice of consciousness or meaningful language. This means that "[h]uman language . . . is the tomb of the animal voice that guards it and holds firm its ownmost essence . . . language is both the voice and memory of death" (*ibid.*: 46).

Relating this to the dialectic of desire and recognition elaborated by Hegel in the "master–slave" dialectic, Agamben perceives a "tight connection" that exceeds a similarity of terminology between the earlier and later texts. He argues that in so far as the "trial of death" undergone by the master or lord entails the renunciation of natural being, the slave's recognition of the master does not amount to recognition as an animal; but nor does it amount to recognition as a true and durable human, since the recognition is unilateral. Rather, the master's "enjoyment" or "satisfaction" is merely fleeting – "Desire has reserved to itself the pure negating of the object and thereby its unalloyed feeling of self ", but consequently, it "lacks the side of objectivity and permanence".[5] For Agamben, the fleetingness or "vanishing" of the master's enjoyment is the "*point at which the 'faculty for death' . . . shows for a moment its originary articulation*" (*LD*: 47, italics in original). Further, in so far as Voice analogously appears as the "originary articulation" of the "faculty for language" but is also the "voice of death", Voice provides the "vanishing and unattainable" point at which the "originary articulation of the two 'faculties' is completed" (*ibid.*). In this way, then, Voice as the originary articulation of language and death must provide for Hegel the negative foundation of the emergence of human consciousness.

While the problem of Voice is, according to Agamben, manifest relatively straightforwardly in Hegel in its characterization as at the point of articulation of death and language in the accession to self-consciousness, the situation is more complex with Heidegger. This is because he does not allow for a simple removal of the animal voice in language, since he already precludes that the animal exists in the same manner as the human. The animal or the living being never experiences the openness of Being that ensures that the human has a unique mode of existence, or *ek-sistence*, as Heidegger puts it, such that the essence of the human cannot be thought from the direction of *animalitas* or as one living being among many: any attempt to do so must remain within the metaphysical approach that Heidegger seeks to overcome. Thus, at this first point at least, Agamben's task seems to accord with Heidegger's, in so far as voice or animal *phoné* cannot provide the starting point for thinking beyond metaphysics. But this does not complete the picture, for Agamben argues that a construal of negative foundation can nevertheless be found in Heidegger's account of *Dasein*, specifically in the analysis of anxiety and the call of conscience.

Heidegger's analysis of *Stimmung* or "attunement" (which finds its most essential expression in anxiety) in *Being and Time* reveals that "between language and voice there is no link, not even a negative one . . . language is not the voice of Dasein, and Dasein, thrown in *Da*, experiences the taking place of language as a nonplace" (*LD*: 57). Thus Heidegger poses the question of a negativity that is more radical, *more originary*, than the negation of Hegelian dialectics and goes on to articulate this in the lecture entitled "What is Metaphysics?" He argues here that *Stimmung* reveals an originary nothingness founded "in a *silence* lacking any further trace of a voice" (*ibid.*). But, Agamben avers, Heidegger does not complete the "interrogation of the origin of negativity" and does not realize the attempt to overcome all reference to voice. Rather, Heidegger's thought reaches a limit that it is unable to overcome, because it understands metaphysics as only involving negativity in relation to voice and thus fails to see that "metaphysics always already construes language and negativity in the most radical context of a *Voice*" (*ibid.*: 58).

The "outer limit" of Heidegger's thought becomes apparent for Agamben in the "sudden reintegration" of the theme of *Stimme* or voice, which the disclosure of *Stimmung* is supposed to have eliminated, in the notion of a call of conscience introduced in *Being and Time* in paragraphs 54–62. For Agamben, the characterization that Heidegger offers entails that the silence or absence of voice revealed by *Stimmung* reverses itself into a Voice, such that the experience of a Voice or *Stimme* is revealed as more originary than that of *Stimmung*, and "through the comprehension of the Voice, Dasein . . . assumes the function of acting as the 'negative foundation of its own negativity'" (*LD*: 59). In fact, Heidegger's characterization of the call of conscience reveals the inextricable connection between Voice and death, since it is only through the call of conscience that *Dasein* is able to think death authentically: as Agamben notes, Heidegger defines the "authentic thinking of death" as an "existential wanting-to-have-a-conscience". Consequently, *"thinking death is simply thinking the Voice"* (*ibid.*: 60, italics in original) and *Dasein* negatively retrieves its own *"aphonia"* in the silent call of conscience.

Agamben continues that the recuperation of the theme of Voice is extended and "completed" in "What is Metaphysics?" In this lecture, Heidegger conceives of a silent Voice of Being, a soundless Voice that calls man to the experience of Being, and to which human language and thought "are born merely as an 'echo'" (*LD*: 60). Granted this interpretation, Agamben thus locates Heidegger's thought within the horizon of the tradition of metaphysics that it seeks to overcome, since it cannot maintain its own project of thinking language beyond every *phoné*, and instead reinscribes the thinking of Being in the negative foundation of the Voice. As Agamben writes,

> The experience of the Voice – conceived as pure and silent meaning and as pure wanting-to-have-a-conscience – once again reveals its *fundamental* ontological duty. Being is the dimension of meaning of Voice as the taking place of language, that is, of pure meaning without speech and of pure wanting-to-have-a-conscience without a conscience. The thought of Being is the thought of the Voice. (*Ibid.*: 61)

While radicalizing the negative foundation of language, Heidegger nevertheless remains within the horizon of metaphysics by locating Being in the place of negativity. The construal of a silent Voice that calls man to the experience of Being is in this sense ultimately analogous to the guarding of the ineffable in language posited by Hegel. Consequently, both remain caught in the metaphysical thinking of *topos* as negativity.

This summary provides us with a clear view of Agamben's diagnosis of the repetition of the presupposition of a Voice that is necessarily and inexorably tied to negativity in the two master thinkers of modern Western philosophy. But it does not tell us what the significance of this is, or why the presupposition of Voice is so apparently problematic. The philosophies of Hegel and Heidegger are respectively directed towards an understanding of the emergence of human self-consciousness or subjectivity and the nature of human being as *Dasein*, that is, not as beings or entities in the world, but as that being that dwells or is properly at home in Being itself. But the upshot of Agamben's argument throughout *Language and Death* is that any such attempt to understand that which is most "proper" to man through reference to negative foundation will fail to do justice to the *ethos* – understood in the Greek sense of the proper dwelling place – of humanity (see *LD*: 94).

More specifically, this metaphysical approach is problematic for two reasons: first, it condemns man "without return and without recourse"[6] to the nihilism of the modern age, an age of "absolutely speakable things" . . . "in which all the figures of the Unspeakable and all the masks of ontotheology have been *liquidated*, or released and spent in words that now merely show the nothingness of their foundation", in which willing "means (*vuole-dire*) nothing" (*LD*: 92). But, crucially, it does so without ever grasping the favourable opportunity that this nihilistic condition presents. Secondly, we have seen throughout that Agamben is concerned with the split established in language between speech and voice, between sign and meaning, between the saying and the said. But the problem goes deeper in that the thought that finds foundation for humanity in negativity establishes and works from an understanding of human *ethos* as split at its origin.

The Presocratic Greek philosopher, Heraclitus, posits at one point that "*Ethos*, the habitual dwelling place of man, is that which lacerates and divides". Citing this, Agamben argues that philosophy has always sought to grasp and "absolve" this split even while that which it has to grasp is "simply a dispossession and a flight"; he writes that philosophy must "always already leave behind its habit, always already alienate itself and divide itself from its habit, in order to be able to return there, walking through negativity and absolving it from its demonic scission" (*LD*: 93, 94). But what if, he asks, the ontotheology of being and its correlative negative foundation of the Voice fails to take the right measure of the *ethos* of humanity; what if that which requires grasping in thought is simply the "mystery" of "humans *having*, of their *habituations*, or their *habits*", such that the dwelling to which we return is not the Voice, but "simply the *trite* words that we *have*?" (*ibid.*: 94). Thus the key concern is not *logos*, as that which articulates and divides being, but simply the having itself.

Ultimately, then, Agamben points towards a path for a new thinking that aims to do justice to the *ethos* of humanity by grasping the simple fact of our "having" language. Within this, overcoming metaphysics does not mean thinking Being as Being (and not simply as beings) – as it does for Heidegger – but thinking language as language, without the negative presupposition of Voice as removed ground and thus without the scission of voice and word, of animal *phoné* and human speech. Or to put the point another way, if we accept the relation of correspondence and identity between the presuppositional structure of Being and language that Agamben posits, then overcoming metaphysics (that is, *thinking*) to the "soil"[7] that nourishes it necessarily requires thinking language as such. From his analysis of Hegel and Heidegger, Agamben concludes that a philosophy that thinks only from the foundation of Voice cannot deliver the resolution of metaphysics that the nihilism towards which we are still moving demands.

Instead, he suggests, this is only possible through an approach that stops thinking from the presupposition of the "supreme shifter" of the Voice and thinks human dwelling in language as such. But, to the extent that the thought of Voice provides the "mystical foundation of our entire culture (its logic as well as its ethics, its theology as well as its politics, its wisdom as well as its madness)", then this cannot provide the basis or foundation for another thinking of human dwelling. Rather, Agamben writes that "[o]nly a liquidation of the mystical can open up the field to a thought (or language) that thinks (speaks) beyond the Voice and its *sigetics*; that dwells, that is, not on an unspeakable foundation, but in the infancy (*in-fari*) of man" (*LD*: 91). That is, it is only by existing "in language without being called there by any Voice" and by dying "without being called by death" (*ibid.*: 96) that humanity can return to its proper dwelling place or *ethos*. This *ethos* of humanity is an experience of "in-fantile dwelling in language", that is, as an experience of *in-fancy*. What, then, does Agamben mean by infancy? It is to this question that I now turn.

The *experimentum linguae* of infancy

Agamben's discussion of the self-reference of language in *Language and Death* draws on his earlier elaboration in *Infancy and History* of the idea of the necessity of an experience in which what is at stake is nothing other than the taking place of language itself. In the extraordinary essay "Infancy and History: An Essay on the Destruction of Experience", Agamben begins his concerted reflection on the concept of experience by reference to Walter Benjamin's diagnosis of the decline in value of experience in the modern world – reflected in the loss of the capacities of the storyteller – and places his own efforts within the programme for a "coming philosophy" that Benjamin outlines elsewhere. In outlining a programme for a future philosophy, Benjamin proposes that this must be centrally concerned with the interrelation of three concepts, namely "epistemology, metaphysics and religion",[8] particularly in relation to the unfinished philosophy of Immanuel Kant. "Unfinished" because, in Benjamin's view, Kant was unable to adequately address the relation between experience and knowledge. In developing a "prolegomena to a future metaphysics", then, the coming philosophy must develop not only a new conception of knowledge but also a new concept of experience.

Of the precepts that Benjamin suggests a future philosophy ought to attend to, one is especially important for grasping Agamben's efforts to fulfil or at least further this programme. This is that, in aiming for a new understanding of experience, the future philosophy must take into account that "all genuine experience rests upon the pure 'epistemological (transcendental) consciousness'", on the condition that the term "consciousness" is stripped of all subjective and psychological connotations and where the "transcendental" consciousness is understood as "different in kind from any empirical consciousness".[9] Directly related to this, the "future epistemology" that this demands should "find for knowledge the sphere of total neutrality in regard to the concepts of both subject and object; in other words, it is to discover the autonomous, innate sphere of knowledge in which this concept in no way continues to designate the relation between two metaphysical entities".[10] One aspect of this is the elimination of any epistemologically significant distinction between intellect and intuition, such that religious experience is as logically possible as "mechanical" or empirically verifiable experience so as to produce a "pure and systematic continuum of experience".[11] With this in mind, we shall see that Agamben's attempt to develop a new concept of experience necessarily and centrally entails engagement with both epistemology and metaphysics, and proposes a radical revision of the subject of knowledge and experience – that is, of the human subject.

To begin his foray into developing a new concept of experience, Agamben claims that the contemporary age is marked by the destruction or loss of experience, in which the banality of everyday life cannot be experienced *per se* but only undergone. He argues that this condition is in part brought about by the rise of modern science and the split between the subject of experience and of knowledge that it entails, and which is extended in modern philosophies of the subject, particularly those that endow subjectivity with psychological substance. For Agamben, the last place in Western philosophy in which the problem of experience was "accessible in its pure form – that is, without its contradictions being hidden" is in Immanuel Kant's *Critique of Pure Reason*, and particularly the splitting off of the transcendental subject of knowledge from the empirical individual (*IH*: 32). Since then, the problem of experience has been increasingly occluded by the repeated attempts to grasp subjectivity as psychological consciousness, and thus unite the subject of knowledge and of experience. Agamben sees this as beginning with Hegel and continuing through the philosophy of Dilthey and Bergson, as well as Husserlian phenomenology, all of which ultimately fail in their own attempts to grasp a notion of pure experience.

Significantly, though, while Agamben posits the destruction or expropriation of experience in everyday life in the modern world, he also maintains that this is not a cause for despair. Rather, in a move that is typical of his thought in which the site of danger or destruction is also the site of salvation, he suggests that the apparent denial of experience may provide a "germinating seed" of a future experience. The novelty of Agamben's approach is that he finds a path to a pure experience through its necessary proximity to language, and, in particular, through what he calls "infancy" or the *experimentum linguae* in which what is at stake are the limits of language itself.

In articulating a new conception of experience, he suggests that this can be found in the experience of "infancy", which in the simplest terms is understood as a wordless, mute condition that necessarily precedes the human being's taking up the position of speaking subject. But instead of simply referencing the neonatal condition as a developmental stage, Agamben's notion of infancy appropriates a now-obsolete meaning of the term, which derives from the Latin *"infans"*, in which *"fans"* is the present participle of *"fari"*, meaning "to speak". Etymologically, then, "in-fancy" means to be unable or unwilling to speak, to be silent or speechless. Thus, while Agamben does on occasion draw on the figure of a newborn child – an infant in the prosaic sense – the condition of infancy does not actually correspond to a developmental stage in human life. Rather, what is important about the figure of the human infant is the way in which the prosaic condition of neonatal humanity highlights that when human beings (understood simply in the biological or zoological sense) are born, they do not speak – they do not have language as a natural capacity, but have to learn and acquire the capacity to speak. Further, it is not determined by the nature of the infant how or what they will speak – that is, the human infant has a capacity to acquire one or more of a large number of languages. For Agamben, this neonatal condition and the necessity of learning to speak show that humans do not have a natural "voice" in the way that animals do. While animals have an immediate relation to voice in chirping, bleating or barking, human beings have no such voice. Instead, they are deprived of voice and must acquire speech; and it is in this need to acquire speech, to enter into discourse, that the experience of infancy subsists.

The importance of the idea of infancy, then, is that it indexes an experience of speechlessness that is internal to the very process of acquiring language, of entering into discourse as a speaking subject. This means that the sense in which infancy precedes our taking the place of speaking subject is not simply chronological but ontological. Agamben's *experimentum linguae* of infancy seeks a pure experience – that is, "something anterior both to subjectivity and to an alleged psychological reality" (*IH*: 37) – that touches on the very "thing" of language itself. To get a clearer picture of what this means, it is worth noting that the term "experience" derives from the Latin root *experiri*, meaning to try or put to the test, which is also the root for "experiment" and for "peril". Thus the *Oxford English Dictionary* notes that to experience something means to make a trial or experiment of it, to put something or oneself to the test, to try or to feel, to suffer or to undergo.[12]

Not out of keeping with these broad senses of "experience", Heidegger, in his essay "The Nature of Language", notes that undergoing "an experience with something . . . means that this something befalls us, strikes us, comes over us, overwhelms and transforms us", indicating that the experience is not "of our own making"; it is not our doing as such that gives rise to the experience that we undergo or that befalls us. Moreover, he goes on to say that "to undergo an experience of language, then, means to let ourselves be properly concerned by the claim of language by entering into it and submitting to it", and "if it is true that man finds his proper abode of his existence in language – whether he is aware of it or not – then an experience we undergo with language will touch the innermost nexus of our existence".[13] These comments from Heidegger are telling in relation to Agamben's idea of an experience of language – it is an experience that we submit to and undergo, and moreover, touches the "innermost nexus" of our being, or what Agamben refers to as the *ethos* of humanity (where *ethos* is understood in the full sense of home or abode). Thus the concept of infancy indicates the possibility of a pure experience wholly based in language itself, which the human subject undergoes, and in doing so, returns to its proper dwelling place or *ethos*.

But two points have to be made about this formulation. First, the experience of language without speech is not an experience we undergo once and for all – which would be the case if infancy were simply chronologically prior to our acquisition of language. We do not simply "return" to the *ethos* of humanity as a lost past that can be recuperated through a different relation to our own infancy. Instead, Agamben insists that the experience of language is one we are always "travelling towards and through" (*IH*: 53) since infancy conditions the very possibility of our taking up the position of speaking subject in any moment of speaking. Recalling the discussion of Benveniste's characterization of pronouns as indicators of enunciation in the previous section of this chapter, we can see that in taking the place of "I" as a speaking subject, the speaker must effectively alienate him/herself as a phenomenal or empirical individual in order to speak – since "I" refers only to the instance of enunciation and not to the individual that speaks "I".

Moreover, in speaking, the individual falls away from the condition of infancy that makes speech possible: by speaking, by entering into a language as a mode of "communicative action", the speaker loses touch with the mute experience of language as such. But this losing touch or fall from infancy does not happen once and for all, since the wordless condition of infancy resides in every utterance; infancy coexists with language and is expropriated or set aside by it in the moment of the appropriation of language in discourse. Infancy conceptualizes an experience of being in language without speech, not in a temporal or developmental sense of preceding the acquisition of language in childhood, but as an ontological condition of speaking that continues to reside in any appropriation of language.

Secondly, and more complicatedly, it is a mistake to think that infancy is an experience the subject *undergoes*, if this is understood to mean that the subject itself precedes that undergoing. Infancy is the experience from which the human subject *emerges*, since it is only in language that the subject has its "site and origin". Thus the recuperation of experience in infancy entails a radical rethinking of consciousness or subjectivity as a question of language rather than of any kind of substantive psychological being. In keeping with Benjamin's exhortation that the future philosophy must base a new concept of experience on a "pure (transcendental) consciousness", Agamben argues that subjectivity can only be understood in reference to its constitution or emergence in language itself. That is, "it is in and through language that the individual is constituted as a subject. Subjectivity is nothing other than the speaker's capacity to posit him or herself as an *ego*, and cannot in any way be defined through some wordless sense of being oneself, nor by deferral to some ineffable psychic experience of the *ego*" (*IH*: 45).

Thus, for Agamben, the mistake of much modern philosophy of the subject is to attribute psychological substance to subjectivity, thereby missing the fact that subjectivity is only a linguistic phenomenon. Subjectivity is only the constitution of consciousness in language through the appropriation of personal pronouns such as "I" and other "indicators of enunciation". In this way, Agamben's approach to subjectivity is both anti-Cartesian and hyper-Cartesian. According to Agamben, the mistake that Descartes made in formulating his famous dictum *"cogito ergo sum"* was to attribute psychological reality to the subject constituted in its own thinking. But Descartes also provides a "glimpse of a future experience of the *ego cogito*", analogous to a vision of "mystical synderesis",[14] in which the *cogito* is "what remains of the soul when . . . it is stripped of all its attributes and contents" (*IH*: 30). Subjectivity for Agamben is understood on the model of a *cogito* stripped of all attributes, thereby finding existence only in its appearance as "I" in language as the medium by which attributes are posited. I shall say more about this understanding of subjectivity in the later chapter on ethics, but for now, what needs to be made clearer is the relation of this conception of subjectivity to infancy and the aim of reaching a new conception of experience.

The first point to note about this interrelation is that if subjectivity is solely constituted in language through "indicators of enunciation" such as the personal pronoun "I", then it follows that a pure or primary experience cannot be an experience *of* the subject – it can only come *before* the subject in a condition of mute infancy or speechlessness. But because "infancy" does not chronologically precede language as discourse but is internal to the appropriation of language in speaking, this means that "we cannot reach infancy without experiencing language" and "the question of experience as derivation of the human individual then becomes that of the origin of language in its double reality of *langue* and *parole*" (*IH*: 48). But because language and the human are inextricably linked – there has never been human being without language and nor is there an identifiable moment in which language emerged – this question of the origin of language must re-interpret the very notion of origin. Without going into the details of this reconception of origin here, it entails abandoning the idea of origin as primary cause or as requiring the identification of "conditions of emergence". Instead, it locates origin in the oscillation between that which has been and the present moment, between the diachronic and the synchronic.

In relation to language, then, infancy is the originary speechless moment that continues to persist in any present moment of utterance. And in existing in the oscillations of the diachronic and synchronic, it is effectively the "engine" that transforms a pure language – the semiotic or *langue* – into speech, that is, human language as the semantic or *parole*. Relating this back to the aim of this essay to find a new concept of experience that is based on a transcendental consciousness stripped of all psychological attributes and existing in language alone, Agamben writes *"in terms of human infancy, experience is the simple difference between the human and the linguistic* [that is, the constitution of the subject]. *The individual as not already speaking, as having been and still being an infant – this is experience"* (*IH*: 50, italics in original). Thus the pure experience that Agamben seeks is the necessary, ineradicable point of transition or oscillation between the human and the subject understood as the constitution of consciousness in language.

One consequence of this conception of infancy as an experience of the oscillation between the human and the subject of speech is that it establishes the human being as a fundamentally historical being; in doing so, it also begins to indicate what we might understand to be the *ethos* of humanity. The fundamental historicity of the human becomes apparent in reference to infancy because the condition of infancy establishes the split between *langue* and *parole*, or between language and discourse, which, Agamben argues, is what distinguishes human language. That is, it is not the case that other animals are deprived of language; quite the contrary, they are always already in language. What is distinctive about human beings is that they must acquire speech; they must alienate their phenomenal individuality in order to appropriate the personal pronoun and become a subject in that moment of appropriation. Agamben writes: "Man . . . by having an infancy, by preceding speech, splits this single language and, in order to speak, has to constitute himself as a subject of language – he has to say I. Thus, if language is truly man's nature . . . then man's nature is split at its source, for infancy brings it discontinuity and difference between language and discourse" (*IH*: 52). Further, "[t]he historicity of the human being has its basis in this difference and discontinuity. Only because of this is there history, only because of this is man a historical being" (*ibid.*). Thus Agamben concludes that "the human is nothing other than this very passage from pure language to discourse; and this transition, this instant, is history" (*ibid.*: 56). While more must be said about the notion of history that Agamben is developing, I set this aside for now and return to questions of history, temporality and origin in Chapter 5. For now, what is important is simply the idea of the fundamental historicity of the human, evident in the conclusive quote from Agamben in which history and the human are identified in the instant of transition between language and discourse.

At this point, one final question can bring our consideration of the notion of infancy to a conclusion: how is infancy not simply a reiteration of negative foundation that Agamben is so critical of in *Language and Death* and to which he opposes the thought of infancy? That is, how is infancy not the ineffable or the unspeakable of the Eleusinian mysteries in another guise? In reference to the project of *Language and Death*, Agamben indicates in the Preface to *Infancy and History* (written in 1988–9 for the English translation) that the notion of infancy is an attempt to think through the limits of language without reference to a "vulgar" notion of the ineffable as that which is outside language – or the element that is "removed" from language in speech – and that provides its negative ground. He writes that because the categories of the unsaid and ineffable belong exclusively to human language, they do not so much indicate the limit of language but the "invincible power of presupposition" in so far as the unsaid is that which must be presupposed in any saying.

In contrast, the concept of infancy "is accessible only to a thought which has been purified . . . 'by eliminating the unsayable from language'" (*IH*: 4). Only this will allow for a real thought of language itself, where "the singularity which language must signify is not something ineffable but something superlatively sayable: the *thing* of language" (*ibid.*). Thus the question becomes: what is the "superlatively sayable" "thing" of language to which Agamben refers? A preliminary response – or at least pointer toward a response – to this question can be found in Agamben's essay "The Thing Itself", in which he argues that the thing itself is not a quiddity or absolute substance behind language but rather "the very sayability, the very openness at issue in language, which, in language, we always presuppose and forget" (TI: 35). Or, to put it another way, the thing itself is the pure communicability that Walter Benjamin argues is necessary for any communication: it is the fact of language itself, not as system of signification or as means of communication, but simply "language as such". I shall discuss this further in Chapter 2. For now, one further dimension of Agamben's engagement with the Western metaphysical tradition requires attention. This is the problem of potentiality, the rethinking of which Agamben takes to be central to the task of overcoming contemporary nihilism.

To be, to speak: actuality and potentiality

As Agamben indicates in the Preface to the English translation of *Infancy and History*, the key task of his work has been to try to understand the meaning of the phrase "I speak". In a later essay, though, Agamben suggests that the subject of his work has been to try to understand the verb "can" – that is "what do I mean when I say: 'I can, I cannot'?" (OP: 177). It may be tempting to see in this revised self-interpretation a shift in focus in Agamben's work, but this would underestimate the deep interrelation of these two questions of "I speak" and "I can"; ultimately, both are addressed to the issue of *potentiality*, or the capacity to do or be (something). There are several ways in which this interrelation can be elaborated: first, given the apparent correspondence or identity between language and being discussed above, it is clear that the question of speaking and being will necessarily overlap in Agamben's theoretical framework. More generally, we can say that there is a necessary logical relation, in so far as the statement "I speak" presupposes that "I can" – that is, the implicit condition of the veracity and indeed possibility of the statement "I speak" is that "I *can* . . . speak".

This formulation suggests that while the question of "I can" addresses a generalized capacity to do or be, the statement "I speak" addresses a specific capacity to do or be something in particular. In this sense, "I speak" would be equivalent to a capacity such as writing poetry, running 100 metres in under ten seconds, or building a house. But as the correspondence between the question of being and the question of language indicates, this would misunderstand the relation between "I can" and "I speak" by simply making one subsidiary to the other. Instead, what has to be kept in mind is that the capacity for speaking has long been seen as essential or definitional for the human in a way that other capacities such as being able to build a house are not – it is by virtue of this capacity for speech that the human being is what it is, distinct from other animals. But as should be clear from the previous discussion, this capacity for speech is not straightforward. Instead, as

Agamben suggests in *Language and Death*, the very nature of this "having" is what needs to be thought. For one, this "having" language or speech necessarily leads to a reflection on the issue of potentiality, since this is at base a question about the *capacity* to enter into speech, that is, the *capacity* to be human. And as the discussion of infancy suggests, this capacity will also entail a privation or incapacity, in so far as speaking entails a simultaneous expropriation in any appropriation of language.

This requires turning to the characterization of potentiality that Agamben develops from Aristotle, particularly in the latter's discussion of potentiality and actuality in *Book Theta* of *Metaphysics*. Aristotle's approach to potentiality and actuality is complex, and Agamben's interpretation is idiosyncratic in its own right, but a brief account of the key elements of each will have to suffice here. Aristotle's discussion of potentiality in *Book Theta* begins with rejecting the position of the Megarians, who argued that something only has potentiality when that potentiality or potency is functioning. For Aristotle, this leads to the absurd conclusion that a man is only a builder in the act of building, and is therefore without the potential to build when he is not building. Similarly, if one is sitting, then one is without the potential for standing, which effectively means that standing is impossible. Against this account, Aristotle defines potency or potentiality as a principle of change by which a thing is acted upon or acts upon itself. Further, in an ostensibly truistic formulation, he argues that a thing is or has potential to the extent that the thing of which it is potential is not impossible.

As simple or banal as that might seem, several complexities are buried within it, and Agamben exploits these complexities to develop his own understanding of potentiality. The first of these is Aristotle's claim that potentiality or capacity must also necessarily imply the *privation* of potentiality or capacity. That is, " 'Incapacity' and 'the incapable' is the privation contrary to 'capacity' . . . every capacity has a contrary incapacity for producing the same result in respect of the same subject".[15] Following on from this, Agamben also emphasizes Aristotle's related point that "that which is capable of being may both be and not be. Therefore the same thing is capable both of being and of not being."[16] For Agamben, the importance of this is that in its essence, potentiality is entwined with its opposite of impotentiality or incapacity; that is, potentiality "maintains itself in relation to its own privation". Agamben writes that "to be potential means: to be one's own lack, *to be in relation to one's own incapacity*. Beings that exist in the mode of potentiality *are capable of their own impotentiality*; and only in this way do they become potential" (OP: 182, italics in original). The relation of potentiality to its own privation is extremely important to Agamben; for instance, with regard to the capacity for speech, this means that such a capacity must necessarily maintain itself in relation to its own privation, its own incapacity. This helps to make sense of Agamben's understanding of infancy, then, since it provides the logical structure by which speaking also recalls and reappropriates the incapacity for speaking in the manner that Agamben sees as characteristic of infancy.

Perhaps most important for Agamben's approach to the problem of potentiality, though, is the claim that "a thing may be capable of being and yet not be, and capable of not being and yet be . . . A thing is capable of doing something if there is nothing impossible in its having the actuality of that of which it is said to have the potentiality."[17] Agamben rejects this standard translation and the interpretation that it gives rise to that "what is not impossible is possible". Instead, he suggests, citing Aristotle, that this is better rendered to mean that "a thing is said to be potential if, when the act of which it is said to be potential is realised, there will be nothing im-potential (that is, there will be nothing able not to be)" (*HS*: 45). Agamben interprets this phrase to mean that "*if a potential to not-be originally belongs to all potentiality, then there is truly potentiality only where the potentiality to not-be does not lag behind actuality but passes fully into it as such*" (OP: 183, italics in original). Hence Aristotle's phrase concerns the conditions in which potentiality is realized; potentiality is not destroyed in the passage to actuality, with im-potentiality set aside or overcome. Rather, the potentiality to not be or do is conserved in the passage to actuality. Agamben writes that "potentiality . . . survives actuality and, in this way, *gives itself to itself*" (*ibid.*: 184, italics in original). Or as Daniel Heller-Roazen explains the point, "actuality is nothing other than a potentiality to the second degree . . . actuality reveals itself to be simply a potential not to be (or do) turned back upon itself, capable of *not* not being and, in this way, of granting the existence of what is actual".[18]

The significant aspect of Agamben's interpretation of this apparently paradoxical statement is the way in which it highlights the suspension or setting aside of im-potentiality in the passage to actuality. But this suspension does not amount to a destruction of im-potentiality; instead, it entails its fulfilment. Agamben claims that to maintain the distinction between potentiality and actuality, and explicate the effective mode of potentiality's existence, it is necessary that potentiality be able to not always pass over into actuality. Therefore potentiality is defined precisely by its capacity to not (do or be) and is thus also "impotentiality" (*HS*: 45).[19] He states that "potentiality maintains itself in relation to actuality in the form of its suspension; it is capable of the act in not realizing it, it is sovereignly capable of its own im-potentiality" (*ibid.*). That is, through the turning back of potentiality upon itself, which amounts to its "giving of itself to itself", im-potentiality, or the potentiality to not be, is fully realized in its own suspension, such that actuality now appears as the potentiality to not not-be. Or, in relation to the capacity to do something, another way to put this point is to say that the potential for doing something is not exhausted in action; rather, the capacity for the act maintains within itself the capacity for not acting, thus maintaining itself in relation to impotentiality or the incapacity for the act.

This portrayal of the relation between potentiality and act has important theoretical consequences for Agamben's conception of political praxis, as I shall discuss later. To get a better sense of the implications more generally of this suspension between potentiality and act here, we can briefly turn to some of Agamben's privileged figures of potentiality. The first of these is the literary figure of Bartleby. Herman Melville's story of the scrivener who refuses to write with the enigmatic phrase "I would prefer not to" has been the focus of a number of philosophical interpretations. What is distinctive about Agamben's approach is his focus on the question of potentiality, impotentiality and the modal operators of necessity and contingency, such that Bartleby ultimately appears as a privileged figure of a "pure potentiality". In a sharp critique of Friedrich Nietzsche's doctrine of the eternal return that draws on Walter Benjamin's portrayal of it as "copying projected onto the cosmos", Agamben suggests that the significance of Bartleby's statement "I would prefer not to" is to break the cycle of "innumerable repetitions" that exhaust all potentiality in actuality.[20] In breaking this cycle, the figure of Bartleby restores potentiality to its relation to contingency by making it possible that something be impossible. Or, more specifically, Bartleby's achievement is to keep "possibility suspended between occurrence and nonoccurrence, between the capacity to be and the capacity not to be" (B: 267). Thus Bartleby thwarts the Shakespearean question of "to be or not to be" by remaining in the (ontological) interregnum of being and not-being, by breaking from the dictates of necessity and will, and wholly residing in the appropriation of an incapacity in capacity. Or, to put the point more pithily, Bartleby does not "not write" but instead manages to "not not-write".

The conceptual importance of the maintenance of a suspensive state between being and not-being is also indicated in the use that Agamben makes of the axolotl, discussed in the short essay "For a Philosophy of Infancy" and elsewhere. Commonly known in Australia as the "Mexican walking fish", the amphibious axolotl is philosophically interesting for Agamben because it remains in a state of neoteny throughout its life. That is, while amphibians typically lose juvenile traits such as gills and gain other characteristics such as lungs and limbs in their metamorphosis into adults (the metamorphosis of tadpoles to frogs being a prime example), the axolotl is remarkable for maintaining juvenile characteristics alongside adult ones.

From the example of an axolotl's remaining in an aquatic larval state even while reaching sexual maturity, Agamben imagines the figure of a child that remains in neoteny, "who so adheres to its lack of specialization and toti-potency that it refuses any destiny and specific environment so as to solely follow its own indeterminacy and immaturity" (FPI). Agamben goes on to say that such a child

> would be thrown outside its self (*gettato fuori di sé*), not as other living beings are, into a specific adventure and environment, but, for the first time, into a world. In this sense, the infant would truly be listening to being and to possibility (*in ascolto dell'essere e del possible*) . . . As the specifically human vocation, infancy is, in this sense, the pre-eminent setting of the possible (*possible*) and of the potential (*potenziale*). It is not a question, however, of a simple logical possibility, of something not real. What characterizes the infant is that it is its own potentiality (*potenza*), it lives its own possibility (*possibilitas*). (FPI)

Agamben goes on to link the figure of the child with his construal of biopolitics as entailing the isolation of bare life within the human, and I shall return to this in later chapters.[21] The important point now is to note the connection that Agamben makes between potentiality and infancy.

What this characterization makes clear is that the condition of infancy discussed earlier as the condition that is expropriated in the human being's appropriation of language is ultimately a matter of pure potentiality. Moreover, in light of Agamben's interpretation of Aristotle, it appears not simply as a condition of "not-speaking", but as one of "not not-speaking". In infancy, the human capacity for speech maintains a relation to its own privation, that is, to an incapacity for speech, which is not exhausted or set aside in the passage to speaking. Rather, it is always and necessarily maintained within the action of speaking, as the ineradicable element that makes speaking itself possible. In this way, then, we can understand why infancy is so important to Agamben in terms of understanding the human "having" of language as speech. But we can now also understand that the experience of infancy that Agamben is seeking is also an experience of pure potentiality, an experience of suspension or *epoché* between speaking and not-speaking. Infancy is a gift in the form of an experience of "not not-speaking" – not simply "*in-fari*" but "*in in-fari*" and the negation of negation in the oscillation of potentiality and actuality.[22]

CHAPTER TWO

Aesthetics: language, representation and the object

Agamben indicates in the 1989 preface to the English translation of *Infancy and History* that the key question that unites his work is what it means for language to exist, what it means that "I speak". In taking up this question throughout his work, and most explicitly in texts such as *Infancy and History*, *Language and Death* and *The Open*, Agamben reinvigorates consideration of philosophical anthropology through a critical questioning of the metaphysical presuppositions that inform it and, in particular, the claim that the defining essence of man is that of having language. In taking up this question, Agamben proposes the necessity of an *experimentum linguae* that allows a new experience of language. As discussed in Chapter 1, this new experience of language is encapsulated in the notion of infancy, which can be understood as a condition that makes speech possible while also being expropriated or set aside in speech. Importantly, this idea of infancy is posed as a way of moving out of the metaphysical presupposition of a negativity inherent to language (which Agamben delineates in the idea of Voice) and, by virtue of that, also inherent to the *ethos* of humanity.

These reflections on metaphysics and the negative ground of language in Voice yield several interrelated avenues for further investigation for Agamben. One of these is to consider the different understandings of language at work in both prose writing and poetry. Following on from his critique of the metaphysical view of language developed in the tradition of Western philosophy, Agamben poses the question of whether the new experience of language that he argues is required can be found in the poetic tradition instead. Focusing on thirteenth-century *Stilnovo* (new style) poetry, he rejects the simple opposition and hierarchy of philosophy and poetry that has structured Western thought at least since Plato. Rather than simply opposing poetry to philosophy and valuing one over the other, he points to a more radical experience of language that has been obscured even by most of the poetic tradition. Ultimately, he argues for a kind of synthesis of poetry and philosophy, which gives rise to an understanding of "critique" as a particular way of knowing. In the first part of this chapter, I discuss Agamben's concerted analyses of poetics and briefly outline his understanding of critique.

Following this, I shift focus slightly to consider more closely some of the epistemological, and ultimately political, implications of the *experimentum linguae*. In particular, I outline the notion of the Idea of language and necessity of appropriating the "thing itself" of language. In the process, I also explore a number of aspects of Agamben's thought, including his philosophy of language and engagement with the linguistic theory of the sign and signified as posed by Ferdinand de Saussure. This provides an opportunity for considering Agamben's approach to language alongside that of Jacques Derrida and thereby gaining a sense of Agamben's divergence from and critique of deconstruction. This discussion also opens into questions about the status of the object, which Agamben takes up in *Stanzas* in terms of a theory of phantasm. As singular as *Stanzas* is as a text – even within Agamben's *œuvre* – it can nevertheless be seen as continuing the project of thinking the relation of "having", which we saw in Chapter 1 is central to Agamben's overall aim of surpassing metaphysics. Drawing on both Freud and Marx, Agamben poses an intriguing analysis of commodity fetishism and object relations in terms of possession and joy, which emphasizes the challenge of appropriating the inappropriable.

In the third and final section of the chapter, I turn to another dimension of the notion of a new relation to objects, that is, in terms of their *production* rather than representation. In this, I outline the contribution that Agamben makes to the philosophy of aesthetics, particularly in his dense but elegant book *The Man Without Content*. In this text, Agamben diagnoses the nihilistic essence of art in the modern era through the fractures and scissions that cross the figures of the spectator and artist. In a damning analysis of modern aesthetics and the attachment to a metaphysics of will that it maintains, Agamben diagnoses a corrosive nihilistic essence in our conceptions of artistic genius and taste. In doing so, he argues for a return to a more originary conception of art that recuperates an Ancient Greek distinction between *poiesis* and *praxis* and restores to the former its relation to truth rather than will.

The experience of language in poetics and philosophy

In Chapter 1, we saw that Agamben's central concern in *Language and Death* was with the perceived tendency in Western philosophy to posit a negative foundation for language, which he calls Voice. Taking Heidegger and Hegel as representative figures for his argument, Agamben shows that both presuppose Voice in their notions of *Da* and *Diese*. The importance of this for Agamben is that any thought that attempts to understand the *ethos* or proper nature of humanity from the foundation of negativity will fail by ensuring that man's nature is essentially a non-nature. The appearance of negativity at the heart of humanity's *ethos* is nihilism, which contemporary thought and *praxis* have, in Agamben's view, failed to overcome or even properly understand (*LD*: xiii). The only way beyond nihilism in this understanding is to conceive of language without Voice; that is, to open thought to a new experience of language that does not presuppose an in-effability or negativity, and instead thinks language as such. The formulation that Agamben uses to typify this new experience is that of infancy, a mute experience that ontologically precedes and conditions the possibility of speech; that is, of the human being's entering into discourse and becoming the subject of speech.

Before arriving at this formulation, though, Agamben poses the question in *Language and Death* whether a new experience of language can be found within the poetic tradition, given its long-standing opposition to philosophy. Since Plato's identification of poetry as the "invention of the Muses", poetry has been seen as a distinctive form and tradition from philosophy, which operates outside or beyond the structure of *logos* and the idea of language as a medium for representing truth-content. Given this apparent divergence, Agamben asks whether there is an extreme experience of language within poetry that does not rest on negative foundation and instead reflects on language's own taking place (*LD*: 66). Focusing on the point of emergence of the modern European poetic form in the Provençal poetry of about the twelfth century, Agamben argues that the key transformation of the troubadour was that "the experience of the event of language is . . . above all [understood as] an amorous experience. And the word itself is *cum amore notitia*, a union of knowledge and love" (*ibid*.: 68). This does not simply mean a "psychological or biographical" event that is subsequently expressed or represented in words; instead, it involves an attempt to render "the event of language as a fundamental amorous and poetic experience", such that love appears as the place (*topos*) of language as such.

Promising as this seems, Agamben nevertheless suggests that the experience of love thus construed "necessarily included a negativity that the most radical troubadours . . . did not hesitate to conceive of in terms of nothingness" (*ibid*.: 69). Because the Provençal poets construed love as unattainable, the experience of language as love is still marked by ineffability and negativity. Hence poetry and philosophy are not opposed as in the Platonic view; instead, they share an understanding of the experience of language grounded in negativity. Importantly, though, this shared understanding of the experience of language's taking place is not an occasion for a full rejection of either poetry and philosophy; rather, it provides the possibility for understanding the scission of poetry and philosophy, and moreover, may also "point beyond their fracture" (*LD*: 74).

Some glimpse of the path beyond the fracture of poetry and philosophy is provided in *Language and Death*, particularly through a reading of the idyll by the nineteenth-century Italian poet Giacomo Leopardi, entitled "The Infinite" (*L'infinito*). Agamben focuses on the role of *deixis* or indication within the idyll, particularly as enacted in the pronoun "this", which is repeated six times throughout. Keeping in mind that pronouns such as "this" indicate nothing other than the instance of discourse itself, Agamben argues that the poem carries out an experience of the taking place of language in this repetition. Even so, the particular experience of language undertaken remains within the philosophical horizon of metaphysics in so far as it appears to assume always that the "this" is universal and negative in much the same manner as that guiding Hegel's analysis of sense-certainty. Moreover, the operation of the temporal shifters of the poem – which move from the past to the future in such a way that the future appears as "having-always-already-been" – means that the poem reiterates the experience of language that is central to philosophy, wherein the taking place of language is unattainable and unspeakable. However, Agamben also glimpses in the last three lines of the idyll a new linguistic experience, which he suggests appears in a contrast between the unattainability of an experience of the place of language and its presence, and which is fully experienced in thought. In this, he suggests, the experience of language ceases to be negative and "the figure of humanity's *having* emerges for the first time in its simple clarity: *to have always dear* as one's habitual dwelling place, as the *ethos* of humanity" (*LD*: 81, italics in original).

This evocative characterization of a new experience of the taking place of language is taken up again and given further articulation in later works such as *The End of the Poem*. The overall project from which this text derives was a proposed attempt on the part of Agamben and others to articulate the fundamental categories that structure Italian culture, and which would reflect on problems of temporality and the transmission of culture, among others (see "Project for a Review", *IH*: 141–50). While never undertaken, this project gave way for Agamben to a more general reflection on themes and problems within poetics. In *End of the Poem*, this is taken up through an engagement with the *questione della lingua*, or question of language, that was central to the Italian Renaissance and revolved around whether literature should be written in Latin or vernacular languages. The transition from Latin to vernacular Tuscan as the national literary language was in large part precipitated by Dante Alighieri's (1265–1321) essay *De vulgaria eloquentia* and by his writing the *Commedia* – now commonly known as *The Divine Comedy* – in vernacular.

One of the problems that emerged from this period of transition, which provides the starting point for Agamben's reflection on the experience of the taking place of language in the *End of the Poem*, is that between a living language and a dead language. The problem of bilingualism that this transition provokes takes an especially emphatic form in an anonymous text, *Hypnerotomachia Poliphili*, in which the Latin lexicon is grafted onto vernacular, thus producing a complex play of lexical and syntactico-grammatical elements (*EP*: 45–6). For Agamben, what is at issue in the *Poliphili* is the love of a dead language. The notion of the death and rebirth of a language, generated by the fifteenth-century humanists' love for Latin, is significant in a number of ways. For one, the notion of a dead language introduces a diachronic split whereby one language is seen as temporally prior to another, living language. Even so, the living language is only intelligible within the context of that which has preceded it, since "only the appearance of Latin as a dead language allowed the vernacular to be transformed into a grammatical language" (*ibid.*: 55). But perhaps more importantly in this context, the idea of a dead language and the love for it contributes to the "dream of language" that is reinvoked "every time a text, restoring the bilingualism and discord implicit in every language, seeks to evoke the pure language that, while absent in every instrumental language, makes human speech possible" (*ibid.*: 60). The provocation with which Agamben concludes this particular essay is whether it may be possible to wake from this "dream of language" such that "there can be human speech that is univocal and withdrawn from all bilingualism" (*ibid.*).

However, later in the text it becomes clear that the wakening from the dream of language cannot be accomplished through poetic experiments such as the reappropriation of dead languages or the formulation of new or pseudo-languages. Exercises in a-grammaticality, onomatopoeia or glossolalia, for instance, are insufficient to disrupt this metaphysical slumber. Agamben makes this point specifically in relation to the Italian poet, Giovanni Pascoli (1855–1912), one of the key precursors to Italian Modernism and the literary experimentation that it entailed. Central to Agamben's interpretation of Pascoli is the latter's claim that the language of poetry is necessarily a dead language, and it is only the death of words that makes thought possible. In Agamben's view, Pascoli's exercises in linguistic forms such as glossolalia and onomatopoeia separate the semantic elements of words from signification to indicate nothing other than the intent to signify, "that is, the voice in its originary purity" (*ibid.*: 67). But, in light of the importance of the death of language, this means that the proper place of poetic dictation is the site at which language can be captured "*in the instant it sinks again, dying, into the voice, and at which the voice, emerging from mere sound, passes (that is, dies) into signification*" (*ibid.*: 70, italics in original). And as should be clear from the arguments of *Language and Death*, this means that rather than achieving a new experience of language as such, Pascoli appears as the metaphysical poet *par excellence*. This is because his is the most radical experience of the metaphysical "mythologeme of the voice, its death and memorial preservation" in language (*ibid.*: 74).

If it is possible to identify anything like a path towards such a new experience of language in poetics, this appears to lie in the metrical character of poetry itself, in so far as its semantic value relies on the (non-coincidental) structural dimensions of both sound and signification. Agamben argues that while it may seem truistic to point out that poetry relies on the "tension and difference" between sound and sense, one of the overlooked consequences of this for an understanding of poetics is the importance of the "end of the poem". Poetry lives in this suspension or non-coincidence of sound and sense, the most concentrated point of which is enjambment, in which the syntactical arrangement continues beyond the end of a line of verse without pause. Importantly, it can and has been argued that enjambment is the singular characteristic that distinguishes poetry from prose. Additionally, though, enjambment highlights the singularity of the end of the poem, simply by virtue of the impossibility of enjambment in the final line of a poem, at its end (*EP*: 112).

This opens the possibility that, at its end, poetry actually fades into prose. But more important for Agamben in these reflections on the end of the poem is the possibility of its opening to a new experience of the taking place of language. He writes:

> the poem falls by once again marking the opposition between the semiotic and the semantic, just as sound seems forever consigned to sense and sense returned forever to sound. The double intensity animating language does not die away in a final comprehension; instead it collapses into silence, so to speak, in an endless falling. *The poem thus reveals the goal of its proud strategy: to let language finally communicate itself, without remaining unsaid in what is said.* (*EP*: 115, italics added)

The emphasis on the notion of a language communicating itself, without remaining unsaid in what is said, makes clear the link between this discussion of poetics and the project of overcoming the metaphysical foundation of language in negativity. It also indicates the way in which the logic of the negation of negation elaborated in relation to the question of potentiality plays out in terms of poetics and the new experience of language: a language communicating itself is a language in which negativity in the form of silence and the ineffable has been negated. At this point, Agamben's discussion of poetics and philosophy touches most directly on the core of his philosophy of language.

Three issues can be drawn out from this conception of language as communicating itself without remaining unsaid in what is said, which help to clarify further Agamben's philosophy of language. The first of these relates to the notion of pure communicability and the mediality of language, which Agamben develops in part from Walter Benjamin. The second relates to Agamben's emphasis on the end of the poem as a path to a new experience of the taking place of language as such, and allows a view of his critical relation to Jacques Derrida's deconstructive approach to questions of language, representation and metaphysics. The third extends both these and relates more specifically to Agamben's discussion of the notion of critique, which he urges as a way of knowing that moves beyond the opposition and hierarchization of philosophy and poetry. For the remainder of this section, I briefly discuss each of these issues in turn.

The idea of language communicating itself goes to the very heart of Agamben's approach to questions of language, speech and representation. If the project of completing metaphysics requires surpassing the tendency to posit the ineffable or silent Voice as the negative ground of language, then another understanding of language must be developed instead. We saw in Chapter 1 that this is closely related to the notion of a new experience of the taking place of language, which Agamben elaborates under the term "infancy". But in outlining this, the focus fell on the *experience* of language, and not specifically on language itself. Infancy is a pure experience prior to subjectivity or psychological reality, which constitutes and conditions language. But to understand this more completely, we now need some clarification of the "thing itself" of language that infancy touches on. This idea of the "thing itself" of language, or the *Idea* of language, is elaborated by Agamben in several essays originally published during the mid-1980s and subsequently translated and republished in *Potentialities*.

The two key essays in this regard, entitled "The Thing Itself" and "The Idea of Language", present a vision of a pure language that is wholly immanent to itself, appearing without scission or unspeakable remainder. In the first of these essays, Agamben returns to Plato's Seventh Letter, in which he tells a story about the Sicilian tyrant Dionysius II, who receives lessons in philosophy from Plato, and the latter's attempt to teach the theory of Forms. In the course of this, Plato posits the "thing itself" as the fifth element of thinking, the other four of which are the name (signifier), *logos* (signified or virtual referent), the object or actual referent, and true knowledge. Rejecting interpretations of this fifth element as a quiddity or obscure *hypokeimenon*, Agamben argues instead that the "thing itself" should be understood in terms of the thing "in the very medium of its knowability, in the pure light of its self-manifestation and announcement to consciousness" (TI: 33). Epistemologically, this is an obscure formulation in its own right. In terms of Agamben's understanding of language, though, it generates the corresponding claim that "the thing" itself of language is the sheer medium of its speakability, that is, "the very sayability, the very openness at issue in language" (*ibid.*: 35). Furthermore, to the extent that this thing of language is always presupposed and "forgotten" in speaking, the task of philosophy is to bring the "thing itself" of language to light, not as a hypothesis among others and not as an ultra-hypothesis beyond or behind all others, but *in itself* or *as such*.

That this is posited as the task of the "coming philosophy" immediately raises epistemological questions about the nature of philosophical knowledge, especially in relation to language. More specifically, it takes us directly to questions about revelation as a mode of knowing, since the thing itself of language cannot be approached through either of the main epistemological traditions in Western philosophy, rationalism or empiricism (since it is always presupposed and forgotten by both). The intimate connection between revelation – paradigmatically expressed in the formula that "In the beginning was the Word, and the Word was God" – and the thing itself is apparent in the second of Agamben's essays mentioned above. He argues that the correct understanding of revelation is that it does not simply entail claims or statements about the world or language but "concerns the fact that the word, that language, exists" (IL: 41) – that is, not *how* something exists but simply that it does. Against the ontological argument presented for the existence of God by Saint Anselm in the eleventh century, Agamben argues that the utterance of the word God – or that than which nothing greater can be thought – does not imply the existence of God but only the existence of the word, that is, language.[1] Thus Agamben affirms the logic of *en arkhē en ho logos*: in the beginning was the word. But, also affirming the refutation of Anselm by the monk Guanilo, Agamben proffers that this word is nothing but voice, which is "no longer the experience of mere sound and not yet the experience of a meaning". Thus "the most original logical dimension at issue in revelation is therefore not that of meaningful speech but rather that of a voice that, without signifying anything, signifies signification itself . . . voice as pure indication of an event of language" (TI: 42). Revelation is then most centrally concerned with voice understood as that which indicates nothing other than the event of language; but the question that remains is whether the reverse implication is correct – that only revelation allows us to comprehend the experience of language.

Interestingly, Agamben contends that the *logos en arkhē* of revelation is in fact the shared presupposition of much contemporary philosophy. However, to the extent that it rests with recognizing this presupposition, contemporary philosophy is condemned to a "marriage with its theological master", since this obscures the true task of philosophy, which is the "elimination and 'absolution'" of all presuppositions (IL: 45). Agamben thus likens the condition of contemporary thought to the image proffered by Ludwig Wittgenstein of a fly trapped within a glass.[2] That is, while contemporary thought recognizes the inevitability of humanity's enclosure within language, it has forgotten the possibility of escape from this condition. To think such an escape requires thinking the limits of language itself, which for Agamben is akin to thinking language itself without sinking into the unsayable or ineffable. And this requires recognition of language as an *immediate mediation*, in so far as, for humanity, it mediates all things and yet is itself immediate: it is the glass through which we see things without seeing it as such. The real task of thought, then, is to think the immediate mediator itself – it is the presentation of "the vision of language itself and, therefore, the experience of language's limits, its *end*" (IL: 47) that must constitute the real task of philosophy.

Both the importance of revelation and the emphasis on language as immediate mediation indicate the importance of Walter Benjamin for Agamben's theorization of the necessity of a new experience of language as such. In fact, Benjamin appears in Agamben's thought as one of the few thinkers who have progressed the task of the coming philosophy beyond the recognition of language as a means of communication and thus the mediating enclosure of humanity. In early essays such as "On Language as Such and on the Language of Man" and "The Task of the Translator", Benjamin elaborates a vision of a pure language that is irreducible to the Babel of multiple languages in effect after the Fall and is intimately related to revelation. As Benjamin writes in the former of these essays, the Fall of language from the divine language of naming inaugurates human language as a means for communicating something other than itself, making it a "mere sign". In contrast to the consequent "mediateness of all communication" that characterizes "the abyss of prattle", the pure language that Benjamin envisages is no longer mediated by meaning: "meaning has ceased to be the watershed for the flow of language and the flow of revelation".[3] As the word of revelation, the essence of which is the name, this pure language communicates nothing other than its own communicability.

Commenting on this idea of a pure language, Agamben asks: "how can human beings simply speak and comprehend speech without the mediation of meaning?" (LH: 53), in response to which he posits the notion of a universal language. By this, he does not mean a grammatical language such as Esperanto, which operates through a "regularization and extreme grammatical simplification" of historical languages. While intended as a form of universal language, Esperanto nevertheless leaves intact the common understanding of language as a system of signs for communicating meaning (*ibid.*: 55). In this way, it is actually a failed universal language, in so far as it excludes the possibility of the fulfilment of languages and relegates it instead to infinite transmission. Instead, Agamben argues that a universal language can only be an *Idea of Language* (*ibid.*: 59), in the Platonic sense of Idea, which "saves and in itself fulfils all languages, and that an enigmatic Aristotelian fragment describes as 'a kind of mean between prose and poetry'" (*ibid.*: 59–60). Or in another formulation, "The Idea of language is language that no longer presupposes any other language; it is the language that, having eliminated all its presuppositions and names and no longer having anything to say, now simply speaks" (*ibid.*: 60).

This formulation of a universal language akin to a Platonic Idea of Language takes us to the second issue to be drawn out from Agamben's formulation of a language that communicates itself without remaining unsaid in what is said. This emphasis on a universal or pure language reveals the distance between Agamben and one of his most important contemporary interlocutors,[4] namely, Jacques Derrida. Despite the ostensible similarity in the philosophical concerns of Derrida and Agamben, the latter is consistently critical of the deconstructive approach championed by the French philosopher. Indeed, he often portrays it as pre-eminently illustrative of the failures of contemporary thought. At issue in the disagreement are two broad questions – the first concerning the status of language in relation to metaphysics and the unity of the sign; the second concerning the consequences of this for interpretation and the future philosophy, that is, the end and closure of philosophy itself.

In his major early works, such as *Of Grammatology*, *Dissemination* and *Margins of Philosophy*, Derrida develops his deconstructive approach to the Western metaphysical tradition, particularly in relation to questions of language. Key for Derrida is the opposition and hierarchy between presence and absence established in the correlative opposition of speech and writing, wherein the former privileges presence, spatial and temporal immediacy and self-evident sense, and the latter is seen as a subsidiary *representation* of speech. For Derrida, Plato is the "father" of the "*logocentric*" hierarchization of speech and writing, and Derrida famously deconstructs Plato's approach to these in the essay "Plato's Pharmakon".[5] In deconstructing the Platonic privileging of speech over writing, though, Derrida's approach is not simply to reverse the opposition, so as to privilege writing over speech.

Instead, deconstruction is premised on showing the impossibility of the distinction itself, because of the mutual contamination of the opposed terms and thus the internal instability of the distinction.

Central to the "method" of deconstruction is the idea of "*différence*" that Derrida develops from the theory of the sign and signification posed by the linguist Ferdinand de Saussure. Taking up Saussure's view that meaning is established in the differences between signs rather than in their relation to an actual referent, *différance* makes undecidability, scission and play the conditions of sense. Derrida writes that, if understood within the strictures of traditional conceptuality,[6] " '*différance*' would be said to designate a constitutive, productive, and originary causality, the process of scission and division which would produce or constitute different things or differences".[7] But, as nothing other than the play of differences, *différance* is ultimately posed as a way of disrupting – although Derrida is explicit that it is not a matter of overcoming – the metaphysics of presence and the concepts of origin, causality and end (in the sense of both *telos* and *eschaton*) on which such a metaphysics is premised. Understood as the "play of differences", *différance* constantly and necessarily defers the "originary", while putting into question the traditional view of the sign as a "secondary and provisional" substitution for presence.[8] Further, *différance* not only pertains to the distinction within language between the signifier and signified; Derrida suggests that *différance* is "*also the relation of speech to language, the detour through which I must pass in order to speak*".[9] Thus the passage from speech to language is itself riven by the play of difference, by deferral and indetermination without end.

In contrast to this, for Agamben, the split established in language by Saussure's distinction between the sign and signifier is fundamentally a part of the tradition of metaphysics. In critical remarks on Derrida's project of establishing a "science of writing" – that is, a grammatology – that takes the sign as its starting point, Agamben argues that "the metaphysics of writing and of the signifier is but the reverse face of the metaphysics of the signified and the voice" (S: 156). Derrida misdiagnoses the problem of metaphysics, in Agamben's view, since its origins lie not merely in the divisions of presence/absence, sensible/intelligible, or signifier/signified. Instead, the key moment is the point of articulation and division itself, particularly as encapsulated in the definition of the human as *zōon logon echōn*, that is, the living being that has language. For Agamben, *logos* is the "fold that gathers and divides all things in the 'putting together' of presence" (*ibid.*: 156). Ultimately, then, what is required is that the "semiological algorithm" of sign and signified must reduce to the very barrier (/) that articulates and divides – not simply as "the trace of a difference" but as the "topological game of putting things together and articulating" (*ibid.*).

The point of this reduction for Agamben is thus not to highlight the endless play of difference, as it might be for Derrida. Instead, the point is to recognize or bring to light a principle of harmony, where harmony is not simply understood in the sense that is familiar to us of a pleasing concord of sounds. Instead, Agamben has in mind a more fundamental and ancient notion of a principle of articulation or tension that preserves difference while establishing unity. He suggests that what is required is a notion of *harmonia* as "the name of the principle itself of the 'just' station or situation in presence". Moreover, it is only "when we have arrived in the proximity of this 'invisible articulation'", he contends, that Western thought might be released from the metaphysics that has long governed our understanding of the sign and language (*S*: 157). Obscure as this idea might seem here, it becomes clearer in relation to Agamben's theorization of community and his revised ontology of identity and difference to be discussed in Chapter 5. For the moment, though, it also alerts us to a further aspect of differentiation between Agamben and Derrida in terms of their understanding of the task of contemporary thought, especially as it relates to themes of end and closure.

As we saw earlier, the end of the poem is a moment of particular significance for Agamben, in so far as it is at the end of the poem that a new experience of language – in which language is communicated without remaining unsaid in what is said – is revealed. By the "end of the poem", then, Agamben obviously does not mean that the poetic form has come to an end, such that no one will any longer write poetry. Rather, the end of the poem refers to those moments that bring a verse or poem to completion. For Agamben, this moment of completion has a particular potency that cannot be limited to deferral and play, but instead halts or suspends the oscillation between speech and voice, between sense and sound. In his deconstructive approach, Derrida resists attributing special significance to an "end" of any kind, emphasizing instead the continuous deferral of both end and origin, in the "play without end" of *différance*. This has the consequence that deconstruction is led to stress the experience of the *aporia*, the moment of irreconcilability that blocks the way or path. For Derrida, it is precisely in this moment of *aporia*, the blocking of thinking, that thinking must take place. Agamben, on the other hand, sees this as a thwarting of the task of contemporary thought. He instead emphasizes the necessity of finding a *"euporic"* resolution of the *aporia*; that is, to find a happy or felicitous path for thinking beyond the *aporia*.

To illustrate this in relation to the end of the poem, the *aporetic* moment is that the final verse of a poem cannot properly be a verse, because of the impossibility of enjambment (which distinguishes poetry from prose). A deconstructive approach might then emphasize the instability of the distinction between poetry and prose, and the necessity of the deferral of the end of the poem – that is, its incapacity to come to an end. Agamben's approach, though, is to find in this *aporia* a moment of resolution that suspends and appropriates the *aporia* itself, such that the "proud strategy" of the poem to let live a new experience of the taking place of language that is no longer predicated on ineffability or silence is revealed. But, additionally, the apparent opposition of poetry and prose is not simply the point of articulation for an ongoing oscillation and indeterminacy; rather, this indeterminacy gives rise to the possibility of a new way of knowing that incorporates aspects of each into itself. Rejecting anything like a prioritization of verse over prose, or poetry over philosophy, Agamben concludes that "perhaps only a language in which the pure prose of philosophy would intervene at a certain point to break apart the verse of the poetic word, and in which the verse of poetry would intervene to bend the prose of philosophy into a ring, would be the true human language" (*LD*: 78).

The name that Agamben gives to this new way of knowing predicated on a "true human language" is "criticism". Agamben argues in *Stanzas* that to the extent that Western culture accepts the distinction between philosophy and poetry, knowledge founders on a division in which "philosophy has failed to elaborate a proper language . . . and poetry has developed neither a method nor self-consciousness" (*S*: xvii). Relating this more specifically to the object of knowledge and the question of representation, Agamben suggests that "poetry possesses its object without knowing it while philosophy knows its object without possessing it" (*ibid.*). Criticism arises at the "extreme point" of this division between philosophy and poetics and its urgent task is to rediscover "the unity of our own fragmented word" (*ibid.*). Criticism is situated at the point at which language is split from itself – in, for instance, the distinction of signified and signifier – and its task is to point toward a "unitary status for the utterance". Consequently, criticism "neither represents nor knows, but knows the representation" (*ibid.*).

While Agamben suggests in the Introduction to *Stanzas* that the one true text of criticism in recent thought is Benjamin's text on *Trauerspiel*, *The Origin of German Tragic Drama*, elsewhere he discusses the work of Max Kommerell, whom he describes in his essay, "Kommerell, or On Gesture", as "certainly the greatest German critic of the twentieth century after Benjamin" (*K*: 77–85). Kommerell is especially significant because his work is thoroughly situated in what Agamben identifies as the third level of criticism: the gestic. Criticism can entail a "philological–hermeneutic" dimension that strives to interpret a work or a "physiognomic" aspect that situates it in relation to its context, or a "gestic" dimension, which is described as resolving "the work's intention into a gesture (or into a constellation of gestures)" (*ibid.*: 77). Importantly, "gesture" is here understood in a technical sense, to isolate the "stratum of language that is not exhausted in communication" and which is "more originary than conceptual expression" (*ibid.*). Gesture, then, is a name for the sheer communicability of language, or speech that has nothing to say or express other than the taking place of language itself. And criticism is the mode of knowing that seeks this experience of gesture as pure communicability. As Agamben writes, "criticism is the reduction of works to the sphere of pure gesture" (*ibid.*: 80). I return to the notion of gesture again in Chapter 5, but for now, two brief points should be noted.

First, it is in this light that Agamben's work entitled *Idea of Prose* might be said to achieve its real importance. Published in Italian in 1985, *Idea of Prose* takes up the question of the distinction between philosophy and poetry through a series of fragments on poetry, prose, language, politics, justice, love and shame, among other topics. This enigmatic text is perhaps especially difficult to understand if read in the way that a philosophical text usually is, for instance, for logical argumentation, for non-contradictory constative claims and veridicality. In the light of the foregoing, though, it is possible to say that what Agamben is doing is performing and indeed undermining a difference between poetry and philosophy by breaking apart and reworking the strictures and articulations of *logos*. In bringing into play various literary techniques such as the fable, the riddle, the aphorism and the short story, Agamben is practically demonstrating an exercise of criticism. In this text, thought is returned to a prosaic experience or awakening, in which what is known is representation itself. Thus the distinction between philosophy and poetry provides the point of departure for a complex exercise of language and representation, experience and *ethos* that Agamben calls criticism.

Secondly, rather than simply being an epistemological exercise in reworking the distinction between poetry and philosophy, criticism has an extreme political importance, which Agamben argues should no longer be ignored. In his two short discussions of gesture – in *Potentialities* and *Means without End* – Agamben takes as a starting point that the modern age has lost its gestures, and because of this, is simultaneously obsessed with them. Evident in literature, poetry, film and elsewhere, the simultaneous loss and hypostatization of gesture reaches its (philosophical and cultural) apex in Friedrich Nietzsche's doctrine of the eternal return, which Agamben describes as a theatre in which gesture is transfigured into destiny. But what is significant about this dual relation of "effacement and transfiguration" of modern humanity to its own gestures is that this renders everyday life increasingly indecipherable or inexplicable. "And", Agamben avers, "once the simplest and most everyday gestures had become as foreign as the gesticulations of marionettes, humanity – whose very bodily existence had already become sacred to the degree that it had made itself impenetrable – was ready for the massacre" (K: 83). In this way, then, Agamben links the question of criticism quite directly to his later theorization of biopolitical sovereignty. More specifically, he makes criticism the political task *par excellence* when he writes, for instance, that "politics is the sphere of the full, absolute gesturality of human beings" (*ibid.*: 85) or "politics is the sphere of pure means, that is, of the absolute and complete gesturality of human beings" (*ME*: 60).

The transfiguration of the object: epistemology and commodity fetishism

Before turning to a discussion of politics as the sphere of gesturality and pure means, it is first important to get a clearer sense of the contribution that Agamben makes to the theorization of aesthetics. One dimension of this to be explored further is the logic of the simultaneous "effacement and transfiguration" of something. While used above to describe humanity's relation to gesture, it is not limited to this. It also provides an apt formula for a more general relation to the object, understood as either the aesthetic object or the object of knowledge. In this section, I elaborate Agamben's proposal for a new relation to the object, which was previously suggested as part of his understanding of criticism, through a brief discussion of some of the central claims of the text *Stanzas*. Somewhat unusual in its engagements with psychoanalytic theory, *Stanzas* nevertheless maintains continuity with the project of overcoming metaphysics through the thought of a new experience of the taking place of language. This is most clear in the later chapters of the book, in which Agamben returns to a discussion of *Stilnovo* poetry, as well as in the concluding discussion of linguistics. But the central thematic of the book – the possibility of new relation to the object – can also be seen as an extended reflection on the notion of "having" that Agamben suggested was a necessary aspect of rethinking the human being's having of language. Within this, the formula that Agamben pursues throughout is the possibility of the "appropriation of the inappropriable".

Agamben's first major contribution to contemporary philosophy of aesthetics was his acclaimed book *Stanzas*, a term that refers to versification in poetry, as well as, in Italian, to rooms, stopping places or spaces of dwelling. In this text, he develops a dense and multifaceted analysis of language, phantasm and the relation to the object, which entails engagement with modern linguistics, psychoanalysis and philosophy. While dedicated to the memory of Martin Heidegger, whom Agamben names as the last of Western philosophers, Agamben's books *Stanzas* also most evidently bears the influence of the art historian, Aby Warburg. The book incorporates research undertaken at the Warburg Institute, and the influence of Warburg's style of art history is borne out in the attention to medieval cultural iconography and cultural categories or typologies. But a substantial part of the book is geared towards innovative interpretations of Sigmund Freud – especially in relation to melancholia and fetishism – and the analyses of Karl Marx and those who followed him, of commodity-fetishism. While moving beyond both Freud and Marx, this generates a vision of a new relation to the object that is no longer predicated on its inaccessibility.

The general frame of Agamben's argument in *Stanzas* is the idea of a new relation to objects, which entails a transformation of the subject–object relation central to Western epistemology, as well as a renewed understanding of possession and hence of pleasure or joy. More specifically, he wishes to elaborate the possibility of understanding the "topology of joy" through which humanity responds to "the impossible task of appropriating . . . [the] unappropriable" and the guiding intuition is that "only if one is capable of entering into relation with unreality and with the unappropriable as such is it possible to appropriate the real and the positive" (*S*: xviii–xix). It is not hard to see the similarities in the notion of appropriating the unappropriable and the idea elaborated earlier of speaking the unspeakable, or bringing into speech the dimension of language that cannot be rendered in words. This conceptual similarity is confirmed, to some extent, in Agamben's treatment of *Stilnovo* poetry in *Stanzas*. But in addition, Agamben finds models for the appropriation of the unappropriable in both melancholia and fetishism.

The importance of melancholia derives from Sigmund Freud's differentiation of it from mourning, on the basis of the relation of introjection and loss that each entails. In his essay "Mourning and Melancholia" Freud argues that while mourning entails the recognition of loss and the transference of the libido on to another object, melancholia is more complicated. The ambiguity of melancholia is twofold: first, rather than transferring to another external object in the face of loss, the libido is subsequently withdrawn into the ego, which is "narcissistically identified with the lost object" (*S*: 19). Additionally, though, it is not clear that there is in fact a loss to which melancholia is a response, or whether melancholia actually pre-empts or anticipates loss. If the latter is the case, then, melancholia is less a "reaction to the loss of the love object as the imaginative capacity to make an unobtainable object appear as if lost" (*ibid.*: 20). For Agamben, the implication of this is that the object that cannot strictly speaking be lost because it is never possessed appears as lost, and thus can be appropriated in so far as it has been lost. Thus the lesson of melancholia is that "the object is neither appropriated nor lost, but both possessed and lost at the same time"; it is "at once real and unreal, incorporated and lost, affirmed and denied" (*ibid.*: 21). This dual status of the object in the melancholic project thus indicates a way into the appropriation of the unappropriable, or the possession of the lost object by virtue of its loss.

For Agamben, fetishism presents a logic that is not altogether dissimilar, because the repetition and substitution of the object of a fetish entails that an unattainable object "satisfies a human need precisely through its being unattainable" (*S*: 33). The fetishist is attracted to a particular characteristic rather than a unique object *per se*, such that any object with that characteristic will satisfy. The object, then, simply stands in for another, always absent object, in much the same way as the poetic device of the synecdoche allows for substitution of a part for a whole. That is, "because the fetish is a negation and the sign of an absence . . . it is something infinitely capable of substitution, without any of its successive incarnations ever succeeding in exhausting the nullity of which it is the symbol" (*ibid.*). The interesting thing about fetishism, though, is that unusual as this perverse relation might initially appear, it is actually an extremely common and everyday experience. This is because it quite accurately describes the role of the commodity in consumerist capital.

In consumerism, what Marx called the "use-value" of an object provides the material substrate of another, intangible, "exchange-value". As Agamben points out, the splitting of value of the material object between something that is useful within the context of some purposive activity, and a commodity whose value is only realized in exchange, transforms the object. It becomes "an essentially immaterial and abstract piece of goods, whose concrete enjoyment is impossible except through accumulation and exchange" (*S*: 37). But in this, the fundamental similarity between the commodity and the object of fetishistic perversion becomes apparent: as with the object of fetish that can never be fully possessed, the commodity cannot be enjoyed as both useful object and an object of exchange-value. In commodity capitalism, the object evokes two contradictory realities, such that "the material body in which the commodity is manifest may be manipulated in all manner of ways, and it may be materially altered so far as to destroy it, but in this disappearance the commodity will once again reaffirm its unattainability" (*ibid.*). Admittedly, Agamben's characterization does not do full justice to Marx's understanding of commodity fetishism. But what is important to note from this is the insight that commodification involves a fundamental "enchantment" and "transfiguration" of the object, in which exchange-value ultimately comes to eclipse use-value.

This transfiguration of the object reaches an apogee in the modern aestheticization of everyday life, which pushes the process of fetishization into a realm where its revolutionary potential can be realized – that is, in the complete appropriation of unreality. Illustrated by Charles Baudelaire's notion of an "absolute commodity" and in the dandyism of Beau Brummell, the completion of fetishization would mean that exchange-value and use-value "reciprocally cancel out each other" and thereby eradicate the commodity that exists by virtue of this distinction. Agamben writes of the dandy that he "teaches the possibility of a new relation to things, which goes beyond both the enjoyment of their use-value and the accumulation of their exchange-value. He is the redeemer of things, the one who wipes out, with his elegance, their original sin: the commodity" (S: 48). At this point, then, the splitting of the value of the object and its consequent production as immaterial in commodification reach their extreme point and pass into the possibility of a new relation to things. This new relation no longer entails the possession of the object as material thing, but allows for the completion and appropriation of the unreal, that is, the making present of that which is absent specifically through the negation of its absence.

In the subsequent chapters of *Stanzas*, Agamben develops his theorization of the possibility of a new relation to the object through poetics and the question of representation. This discussion, which is an important background and corollary to the arguments developed in *The End of the Poem*, understands the object relation in a more epistemological register; that is, as the object of knowledge and representation. Alongside a theory of phantasm, Agamben finds promise in the characterizations of love proffered in *Stilnovo* poetry, and especially in Dante. In this, the torsions of the distinction between poetics and philosophy (the love of wisdom) give rise to the notion of criticism that I discussed earlier. These reflections thus pose the relation to an object in terms of possession and representation, which Agamben associates with joy or happiness. However, there is another dimension of the relation of humanity to objects, which Agamben takes up elsewhere. This is the nature of the object's *production*, which should be understood not simply in terms of the means of production (how something is made), but in terms of the nature of production itself. In this sense, the question of humanity's relation to the object opens into questions about *poiesis* and *praxis* as modes of human action.

The nihilistic essence of aesthetics: *poiesis* and *praxis*

Initially published in 1970 and republished in 1994, *The Man Without Content* is effectively Agamben's first book-length study. Unlike later texts, the book is written in a manner that is largely consistent with traditional philosophical stylistics. At the same time, the conceptual influence of Heidegger is unmistakeable throughout Agamben's perspicacious readings of several master figures of Western philosophy such as Aristotle, Kant, Hegel and Nietzsche. The text focuses on philosophy of aesthetics and heralds Agamben's critical relation to metaphysics, which is extended and deepened in *Language and Death* and elsewhere. The text also presages Agamben's critique of philosophical approaches to subjectivity that attribute psychological content to the subject, a project that is extended and modified through texts such as *Infancy and History* and *Remnants of Auschwitz*. But the text is also important in itself for its damning critique of modern aesthetics, and for its discussion of *poiesis* and *praxis* in relation to art.

The overall project of *The Man Without Content* is to illuminate the consequences of the "self-annihilation" of art in the modern era, which entails attempting to understand or bring to light the link between aesthetics and nihilism. Agamben begins by identifying the "double principle" of modern aesthetics, which revolves around the disinterestedness of the spectator on the one side, and the dangerous interest of the artist as creator on the other. That is, in modern aesthetics "to the increasing innocence of the spectator's experience in front of the beautiful object corresponds the increasing danger inherent in the artist's experience" (*MWC*: 5). In the history of philosophy, this duality of principles is expressed in Kant's emphasis on disinterested aesthetic judgement and Nietzsche's subsequent critique of this and emphasis on the creative will of the artist. For Agamben, rather than being opposed, these two positions illuminate the "speculative centre and . . . vital contradiction" (*ibid.*: 12) of the history of aesthetics. The consequence of this is that the "original unity of the work of art" is broken apart, leaving a schism between the dual principles of aesthetics in which no foundation can be found for either, but each is constantly referred back to the other. The problem that Agamben poses for himself, then, is to seek foundation for each of these principles – of aesthetic judgement and artistic subjectivity – for themselves rather than in the constant oscillation between them.

In tracing the splitting of these principles, Agamben isolates the emergence of the figure of the "man of taste" in the mid-seventeenth century as a crucial vector in the genealogy of modern aesthetic sensibility.[10] The man of taste, he argues, is seen as having a capacity to identify and appreciate the point of perfection in an artwork. Correlatively, the more refined the spectator's sensibilities, the more the artist "moves in an increasingly free and rarified atmosphere" (*MWC*: 16). One consequence of the delicacy of this sensibility, then, is that it comes at the cost of the capacity to produce art itself. An extreme example of this can be found in Diderot's figure of

Rameau's Nephew, who is endowed with "the ability to judge but not the ability to create" and in whom "taste has worked like a sort of moral gangrene, devouring every other content and every other spiritual determination", ultimately exerting itself "in a total void" (*ibid.*: 23). Rameau's nephew exemplifies the splitting of the capacity for aesthetic judgement in the spectator from the creative genius of the artist and, as such, he is the apogee of the man of taste; however, according to Agamben, in this splitting of taste from genius "taste becomes a pure reversal, that is, *the very principle of perversion*" (*ibid.*: 24, italics in original). This is not to say that there is a simple indeterminacy between good and bad taste; rather, as the principle of perversion itself, good taste leads to a condition of self-alienation and dispossession such that the consciousness of the man of taste is "radical inconsistency" and his "fullness is absolute lack" (*ibid.*: 26). Further, for Agamben, the possible link between aesthetics and the condition of European nihilism now becomes apparent, for the figure of the man of pure taste is correlative with the destruction of social values and religious faith; consequently, the "destiny of art" must be understood in the context of the rise of nihilism.

Taking up the question of the destiny of art in relation to aesthetic judgement, particularly in so far as it has given rise to the "critic" as a specific profession and character, Agamben argues by way of Kant that the key but obscured aspect of aesthetic judgement is that as much as it tries to determine the beautiful, it can do so only negatively. For Agamben, the true object of aesthetic judgement is not art *per se*, but only what it is not; that is, its shadow or non-art. In this way, "our appreciation of art begins necessarily with the forgetting of art" (*MWC*: 43) and art is grasped only as negativity. Criticism is necessarily ruled over by the *logos* that folds together art and its shadow of non-art, and any attempt to get beyond this condition must therefore enquire after the foundation of aesthetic judgement itself. While modern thought has consistently failed in its attempts to grasp the foundation of aesthetic judgement, Agamben poses the possibility that judgement is today undergoing a crisis that may in fact lead to its eclipse. This eclipse is evident in two tendencies today, the first of which is the production of art objects such as Marcel Duchamp's ready-mades for which the polarities of art/non-art are wholly inadequate as conceptual schemas. The second is the increasing aestheticization of nature, such that while it has historically been excluded from aesthetic judgement, nature is increasingly compared with its shadow and subjected to the appreciation of the "point of perfection" that characterizes taste.

Occurring alongside this encompassing of the world by the perverse principles of taste and the consequent indeterminacy of art and nature, though, is another process, namely, the emptying of artistic subjectivity of any content. In tandem with the purification of taste and consequent self-alienation of the spectator, the artist also undergoes a fundamental transformation in the modern era. Agamben points out that in contrast with the modern propensity for the collection of art and thus its isolation from human dwelling in the world, in the Middle Ages the object of artistic production was considered so closely intertwined with the subjectivity of the artist that it was impossible to consider the object has having value in itself. But, he argues, this immediate unity of artist and material was broken, in part because of the rise of aesthetic judgement. The best diagnosis of the consequences of the subsequent split of artistic subjectivity from the material of artistic production is Hegel's, in his *Lectures on Aesthetics*. Hegel argues that since it is now unconstrained by any immediate relation between the artist and his material, art becomes a domain of freedom that "seeks its end and its foundation in itself" (*MWC*: 35).

At the same time, this entails that there is an absolute diminution of the significance of content in art. As Hegel writes, "No content, no form, is any longer immediately identical with the inwardness, the nature, the unconscious substantial essence of the artist; every material may be indifferent to him if only it does not contradict the formal law of being simply beautiful and capable of artistic treatment".[11] It is in this way, then, that the artist appears as "the man without content", as a figure without any substantive relation to the objects of art he produces beyond the formal values of aesthetic perfection. The appearance of the artist as the man without content has damning implications for art in this view, for it leads to a fundamental and radical split in the consciousness of the figure of the artist that corresponds to that within the spectator. Having been divorced from any content, the artist "finds himself in the paradoxical condition of having to find his own essence precisely in the inessential, his content in what is mere form" (*MWC*: 54). Further, art ultimately appears as a "self-annihilating nothing", or a negation that negates only itself. But this does not mean that art ends or dies as such; rather, art endlessly "survives beyond itself", but only in a nihilistic *terra aesthetica* of empty forms and contents. And, for Agamben, the destiny of art cannot be decided upon until the "secret" nihilistic essence that rules Western thought, which condemns humanity to negation and Nothingness, is brought to light.

Given this diagnosis of the nihilistic essence of art, the remaining chapters of this book are dedicated to an attempt to bring forth a more originary understanding of art or at least to clear away some of the confusions that currently reign and prevent such an understanding. In this, Agamben focuses on the notion of *poiesis*, or creative production. According to him, the question of the destiny of art touches on a fundamental question about human nature in so far as human nature is defined as *poetic*, where poetry does not simply name one form or art among others, but is "the very name of man's doing", that is, of "*pro-ductive action*" (MWC: 59, italics added). Thus the question that needs to be addressed is: "[w]hat does it mean that man has on earth a poetic, that is, a pro-ductive, status?" (*ibid.*). The first thing to note about this definition of man's nature is simply that it means that man's "dwelling on earth" is *practical*; but whereas we are now accustomed to thinking of all practical activity in a unified fashion, Agamben wishes to retrieve a more differentiated understanding of man's productive nature through returning to the ancient Greek distinction between *poiesis, praxis* and work.

In the eighth chapter of *Man Without Content*, Agamben proffers an analysis of the concepts of *poiesis* and *praxis* that attempts to shake off the confusions with which they are beset in Western thought, and in doing so, retrieve some of the original philosophical significance of *poiesis*. He points out that the Greeks understood *poiesis* as making, or a form of activity characterized by bringing something into being; that is by "the fact that something passed from nonbeing to being, from concealment into the full light of the work" (MWC: 68–9). Thus the defining characteristic of *poiesis* lay in its "being a mode of truth understood as unveiling" (*ibid.*: 69). In contrast, *praxis* was understood in the sense of "to do", and as such was fundamentally related to the will and its immediate realization in an act. Third and least valuable in this tripartite distinction is work. While not addressed thematically as one of the fundamental human modes of action, work was nevertheless important for the Greeks for its immediate relation to biological life and the reproduction of the conditions of vital existence.

According to Agamben, the differentiation and hierarchic valuation of *poiesis, praxis* and work has been obscured throughout the history of Western thought, reaching its completion in the modern era. Today, all distinction between *poiesis* and *praxis* is lost and, moreover, work comes to be seen as having the highest value. In this the particular sense of *poiesis* as a mode of truth as unveiling is lost, and is instead melded into a notion of *praxis* as willed activity. Further, in an analysis that recalls (though does not simply repeat) that of Hannah Arendt,[12] Agamben places the burden for the reversal of the modes of human activity with Karl Marx's valorization of labour and work, which defines man as the animal or living being that produces and works. The consequences of these transformations are, first, that *poiesis* is overridden by a notion of creative genius, whereby the work of art is seen as an expression of the will of the artist (MWC: 70). Further, alongside the valorization of work, *praxis* comes to be rooted in biological existence, through an emphasis on the vital impulses and passions of man as a natural being (*ibid.*: 71). Agamben avers that while the value of Marx's thought lies in his recognition of *praxis* as an *original* characteristic of man in the sense that it holds together and founds man as man, he nevertheless fails to overcome the metaphysical horizon of Western thought (*ibid*.: 83–4). This is because not only does Marx retreat from his insight into *praxis* as an original characteristic of man into a "naturalistic connotation of man as natural being", he also continues to emphasize a metaphysics of will. As Agamben writes, in this view, "the original container of the living being 'man', of the living being who produces, is will" (*ibid*.: 85).

This takes us to the heart of the problem with modern aesthetics. For rather than understanding *poiesis* in a more original way as unveiling, modern aesthetics also continues to be wedded to the metaphysics of will. Just as our understanding of *praxis* has started from confusion, so all attempts to transcend aesthetics have also started with the blurring of *poiesis* and *praxis*. In this, art has been understood as a mode of *praxis* understood as "the expression of a will and a creative force" (*MWC*: 71). Agamben writes, "the point of arrival of Western aesthetics is a metaphysics of the will, that is, of life understood as energy and creative impulse" and, as such, is founded in "the forgetting of the original pro-ductive status of the work of art as foundation of the space of truth" (*ibid*.: 72). This tendency can be diagnosed as much in Novalis's definition of poetry as active, wilful and productive as in radical projects that emphasize the liberation of creative will and impulse. But it reaches its apex in Nietzsche's doctrines of eternal recurrence and art as will to power, which Agamben portrays as "the furthest point" of the "metaphysical itinerary" of aesthetics. We do not need to follow the details of this analysis here. But the upshot of it is that, ultimately, all critiques that maintain vestiges of the idea of art as the expression of the creative impulse and genius of the artist are condemned to repeat the metaphysics of will and, in doing so, ensure the nihilistic power – as a "self-annihilating nothing" – of art in the modern era.

While Agamben disavows any easy resolution of the nihilism of Western aesthetics, concluding the book with the admission that it is impossible to say whether a more original conception of *poiesis* may be attained, or whether art may once again take "the original measure of man on earth" (*MWC*: 103), he nevertheless seems to indicate some direction for further reflection on the problem. The final chapter is dedicated to a dense reflection on rhythm, which he argues "grants men both the ecstatic dwelling in a more original dimension and the fall into the flight of measurable time" (*ibid*.: 100). Following a cryptic comment by the German lyric poet Friedrich Hölderlin on the relation of rhythm and art, Agamben suggests that the suspensive temporality of rhythm may point the way beyond an aesthetics of disinterested taste and creative will. In short, he suggests that rhythm promises to open man to an epochal temporality that breaks apart the continuum of linear time, and in doing so, makes possible access to a more original understanding of the work of art. He writes:

> [t]o look at a work of art, therefore, means to be hurled out into a more original time: it means ecstasy in the epochal opening of rhythm, which gives and holds back. Only by starting from this situation of man's relationship with the work of art is it possible to comprehend how this relationship – if it is authentic – is also for man the highest engagement, that is, the engagement that keeps him in truth and grants to his dwelling on earth its original status.
>
> (MWC: 102)

While this brief discussion barely hints at it, Agamben's focus on rhythm as epochal opening suggested in this quote points to the importance of *time* within his project. More specifically, it highlights the perceived importance of breaking apart the continuous passage of measurable time in a more originary temporality. While this concern is carried through in texts such as *Infancy and History*, in which Agamben emphasizes the political necessity of a more radical conception of time as epochal, this is brought to fuller fruition in a recent text, *The Time that Remains*. Here Agamben provides the clearest articulation of a suspensive *messianic* time that breaks apart the notion of time as a continuity of instants.

Before turning to his conception of messianic time, though, it is first necessary to get a clear sense of Agamben's diagnosis of contemporary democracy and biopolitics. As I suggested earlier, one of the key dictums around which Agamben's thought circles is Aristotle's definition of man as the being that has language and who can therefore decide on the just and the unjust. By this, he means that it is by virtue of having language that man is a political animal. While we have so far focused on the relation of having by which man and language are linked, it is also necessary to consider the consequences of the formulation of man as the political animal; that is, as the being who finds his *ethos* or proper being in the *polis* or place of politics. It is on the basis of this linkage that Agamben builds his critique of democracy as a form of exceptional politics rooted in the biological life of man.

CHAPTER THREE

Politics: biopolitics, sovereignty and nihilism

In what is perhaps his best-known book, *Homo Sacer*, Giorgio Agamben takes up the concept of biopower proposed by Michel Foucault to provide a radical reinterpretation of the modern political condition as one of legal abandonment and nihilism. In the final chapter of *The History of Sexuality*, Foucault argues that the regime of power that emerged from the seventeenth century onwards involved a fundamental reversal of the principle of power's operation.[1] He claims that whereas sovereign power operated on the principle of the right to commit its subjects to death in order to enhance the strength of the sovereign, modern power reverses this axis and works through the administration of life. The entry of life into the mechanisms of power and correlative organization of political strategies around the survival of the species constitutes the "threshold of modernity" for Foucault.

The historical claim that biopolitics emerged during the seventeenth century provides the point of purchase of Agamben's own critical thesis on biopolitics, which he describes as an attempt to "correct or at least complete" Foucault's analysis of the relation between biopolitics and sovereign power. Agamben claims that rather than being characteristic of the modern era, biopolitics and sovereignty articulate in a much more fundamental way, such that the "production of a biopolitical body is the original activity of sovereign power" and "biopolitics is at least as old as the sovereign exception" (*HS*: 6). As this suggests, the political status and function of the legal exception is central to Agamben's analysis of biopolitics, and it is this that allows him to identify the contemporary condition as one of abandonment and nihilism. As we shall see, it is through the exception that sovereignty and life are brought into conjunction; in other words, it is the exception that founds sovereign power, and allows the law to take hold of life.

In developing his critical analysis of Foucault's historico-theoretical thesis on biopolitics and sovereignty, Agamben makes a number of significant conceptual shifts away from Foucault. For one, Agamben's heritage is not so much the Nietzschean emphasis on relations of force that informs Foucault's genealogical approach but the ontological concerns of Aristotle and Heidegger, even though each of these is critically reformulated in his work. Consequently, the historiographical commitments of Foucault and Agamben are also strikingly at odds: while Foucault's genealogy rejects the search for origins and instead traces the emergence of particular configurations of relations of force, Agamben seeks to illuminate the "originary" relation of law to life. In this attempt, Agamben's account of biopolitics is driven by a decisive engagement with the work of Walter Benjamin on the one hand and Carl Schmitt's theory of sovereignty on the other. In fact, his account of biopolitics is more accurately read as an attempt to fulfil or complete Benjamin's critique of Schmitt's theory of sovereignty than it is an attempt to "complete" Foucault. To a large extent, Benjamin provides Agamben with the theoretical resources to think beyond the state of exception articulated by Schmitt in his decisionistic account of sovereignty, which Agamben sees as symptomatic of the nihilistic "form of law" in operation in modernity. In this chapter, I focus on two aspects of Agamben's more explicitly political thought: his conception of sovereignty and the exception, and his understanding of the interrelation of life and law in the notion of "bare life". Throughout the discussion of each of these, I begin to outline the influence of Benjamin and the import of this for Agamben's engagement with Schmitt in particular. I also specify Agamben's relation to his contemporaries, such as Antonio Negri, and French thinkers such as Foucault and Gilles Deleuze. This chapter explicates the central theses of Agamben's political theory, providing the necessary background for a more critical engagement in subsequent chapters.

Sovereignty and the exception: diagnosing biopolitics

Foucault developed his analysis of biopolitics as a new form of power in lecture series in the early to mid-1970s, culminating in the oft-cited characterization in the first volume of *History of Sexuality*. Here, he argues that the eighteenth century witnessed an event nothing short of the engagement of life in history, that is, "the entry of phenomena peculiar to the life of the human species into the order of knowledge and power, into the sphere of political techniques".[2] He goes on to claim that "for the first time in history, no doubt, biological existence was reflected in political existence".[3] Thus the administration of life has become the central characteristic and defining rationale of the regime of power operative in the modern world. From this,

Foucault suggests that the conception of man proposed by Aristotle as a "living animal with the additional capacity for a political existence" should be revised to acknowledge that "modern man is an animal whose politics places his existence as a living being in question".[4] Agamben revisits this Aristotelian definition of man in his own account of biopolitics, to suggest that the ancient distinction between *bios* or political life, and *zoē*, or biological life, is at the bottom of the current biopolitical condition. It is this distinction between different modes of living that allows for the production of the biopolitical subject – that is, bare life. In this way, Agamben resists the reversal of political and biological life that Foucault diagnosed as the "threshold of modernity" and, instead, proposes an intrinsic or "originary" relation between law and life established through the exceptional structure of sovereign power.

The starting point for Agamben's discussion of biopolitics in *Homo Sacer* is the apparent paradox of sovereignty, wherein the sovereign is simultaneously inside and outside the juridical order, a situation encapsulated in the notion of the "sovereign exception". Taking up Carl Schmitt's decisionistic thesis that the "sovereign is he who decides on the exception",[5] Agamben argues that what is at stake in the state of exception is the very possibility of juridical rule and the meaning of state authority. According to Schmitt, in deciding on the state of exception – a process in which the sovereign both includes and excludes itself from the purview of law – "the sovereign 'creates and guarantees the situation' that the law needs for its own validity" (*HS*: 17). He argues that since the exception cannot be codified in the established order, a true decision that does not rest on a pre-existent norm or rule is required in order to determine whether it is an exception and, thus, whether the rule applies to it. Sovereignty resides in this decision on what constitutes public order and security, and, hence, whether the social order has been disturbed. He claims that "the exception is that which cannot be subsumed; it defies general codification, but it simultaneously reveals a specifically juristic element – the decision in absolute purity . . . Therein resides the essence of the state's sovereignty, which must be juristically defined . . . as the monopoly to decide."[6] Further, because the sense of the legal order rests upon the existence of the normal situation, the form of the sovereign decision is a decision on the norm and the exception. Thus sovereignty is the "border-line concept" of order and the exception, where the sovereign decides whether the situation that confronts it is truly an exception or the normal order, such that sovereignty itself becomes apparent in that decision.

In his interpretation of Schmitt, Agamben takes up the notion of the sovereign as borderline or limit concept to argue that the defining characteristic of sovereignty is that the sovereign determines when law is applicable and what it applies to, and, in doing so, must also create the conditions necessary for law to operate since the law presupposes normal order for its operation. As Agamben states, "what is at issue in the sovereign exception is not so much the control or neutralization of an excess as the creation and definition of the very space in which the juridico-political order can have validity" (*HS*: 19). The sovereign thus operates as the threshold of order and exception, determining the purview of the law. This means that the state of exception is not simply the chaos that precedes order. For Agamben, it operates both as a condition of law's operation and an effect of the sovereign decision such that the exception is not simply outside the realm of the law, but is in fact created through the law's suspension. The sovereign determines the suspension of the law *vis-à-vis* an individual or extraordinary case and simultaneously constitutes the efficacy of the law in that determination.

But Agamben adds the caveat that while the law might be suspended in relation to the exception, this does not mean that the exception is without relation to the rule; rather, the state of exception is such that what is excluded from the purview of the law continues to maintain a relation to the rule precisely through the suspension of that rule. That is, the exception is included within the purview of the law precisely through its exclusion from it.[7] The effective consequence of this is that the exception confirms the rule by its being other than the normal reference of the rule. Agamben concludes from this structure of the exception that "the rule applies to the exception in no longer applying, in withdrawing from it" (*HS*: 18). With regard to juridical rule, then, the state of exception that characterizes the structure of sovereignty is not simply inaugurated through an interdiction or confinement, but through the suspension of the validity of the juridical order, wherein the rule withdraws from the exception and applies to the exception in that withdrawal. As Agamben states, "[t]he exception does not subtract itself from the rule; rather, the rule, suspending itself, gives rise to the exception and, maintaining itself in relation to the exception, first constitutes itself as a rule. The particular force of law consists in this capacity of law to maintain itself in relation to an exteriority" (*ibid.*).

Following Jean-Luc Nancy, Agamben suggests that the term most appropriate to the capacity of the law to apply in no longer applying is that of the ban (*HS*: 28). That which is excluded is not simply set outside the law and made indifferent or irrelevant to it, but rather abandoned by it, where to be abandoned means to be subjected to the unremitting force of the law while the law simultaneously withdraws from its subject. As Nancy states, "the origin of 'abandonment' is a putting at *bandon*", where

[b]andon is an order, a prescription, a decree, a permission and the power that holds these freely at its disposal. To abandon is to remit, entrust, or turn over to such a sovereign power, and to remit, entrust, or turn over to its ban, that is, to its proclaiming, to its convening, and to its sentencing . . . the law of abandonment requires that the law be applied through its withdrawal . . . Abandoned being finds itself deserted to the degree that it finds itself remitted, entrusted, or thrown to this law.[8]

Agamben claims from this that the position of being in abandonment correlates to the structural relation of the exception: "the relation of exception is a relation of ban" (HS: 28). Just as with the exception that is included only through its exclusion, the subject of the ban is not simply excluded from the realm of the law, set outside and untouched by it, but is given to the law in its withdrawal. This correlation between the exception and abandonment means that it is impossible to say clearly whether that which has been banned is inside or outside the juridical order (ibid.: 28–9).

Taking his cue from both Benjamin and Schmitt, Agamben argues in Homo Sacer that what is captured within the sovereign ban is life itself. He states that "life . . . [is] the element that, in the exception, finds itself in the most intimate relation with sovereignty" (HS: 67). Or again, since the "law is made of nothing but what it manages to capture inside itself through the inclusive exclusion", it finds its own existence in the "very life of men" (ibid.: 27). Further, in the state of exception, the law effectively coincides with life itself, such that fact and norm enter into indistinction, and the form of law can be understood as "being in force without significance".[9] Addressing a disagreement between Benjamin and Judaic scholar Gerschom Scholem on the status of law in Franz Kafka's writings,[10] Agamben argues that the formulation "being in force without significance" proposed by Scholem perfectly describes the status of law in the state of exception. Agamben takes this phrase to describe the situation in which "the law is valid precisely insofar as it commands nothing and has become unrealizable" (MS: 172). In being in force without significance, the law is not absent, but is emptied of positive content or meaning, and suspended in its application. It is not that the law no longer applies as in a state of lawlessness; rather, while applying, the law cannot do so in any concrete or immediate sense since it has lost any apparent meaning or intelligibility.

But in taking up Scholem's phrase, Agamben also proposes that he misses the fundamental importance of Benjamin's objection that the law that has lost all content is indistinguishable from life (HS: 53). By the indistinguishability of life and law, Benjamin appears to mean that the law is reduced to the ontic conditions of existence and cannot rule over life through claims to transcendence. Correlatively, there is no possibility of interpretation of the law from the position of life, since life is itself indistinguishable from law.[11] Agamben concludes from these opposed positions that there is an essential correlation between life under a law in force without significance and life in the sovereign exception, in that neither situation allows that life and law be distinguished: in the state of exception, law without significance passes into life while life always subsists in relation to the law.

Importantly, Agamben is not simply suggesting that natural or biological life founds the existence of law. Rather, the key figure in the inclusive exclusion is bare life, understood as the "zone of indistinction" or hinge through which political and natural life articulate. For Agamben, bare life arises because "human life is politicized only through an abandonment to an unconditional power of death" (*HS*: 90). As he states, "not simple natural life, but life exposed to death (bare life or sacred life) is the originary political element" (*ibid.*: 88). Agamben notes that the qualitative distinction made by Aristotle in his treatise on the formation of the state between biological life (*zoē*) and political life (*bios*) effectively excluded natural life from the *polis* in the strict sense and relegated it entirely to the private sphere, as the basic life of reproduction.[12] The category of bare life emerges from within this distinction, in that it is neither *bios* nor *zoē*, but rather the politicized form of natural life. Immediately politicized but nevertheless excluded from the *polis*, bare life is the limit-concept between the *polis* and the *oikos*. And in being that which is caught in the sovereign ban, bare life indicates the exposure of natural life to the force of the law in abandonment, the ultimate expression of which is the sovereign's right of death. Thus, neither *bios* nor *zoē*, bare life emerges through the irreparable exposure of life to death in the sovereign ban. I return to a more extensive discussion of the notion of "bare life" in the following section, but first I want to make several further points about Agamben's account of biopolitics and sovereignty.

Agamben's return to Aristotle to describe the foundations of Western politics has several implications worth mentioning. First, it allows him to argue that bare life is not a modern invention but, instead, stands in an originary relation with Western politics. Hence, in a provocative formulation, he suggests that "in Western politics, bare life has the peculiar privilege of being that whose exclusion founds the city of men [*sic*]" (*HS*: 7). Secondly, this claim indicates the tight integration between sovereign power and biopower that Agamben sees in contrast to the historical succession of sovereignty and biopower that Foucault at least appears to posit at times.[13] Against Foucault, Agamben claims that bare life has long been included in Western politics as the "original – if concealed – nucleus of sovereign power", such that biopolitics and sovereignty are originally and fundamentally intertwined. This means that modern politics does not represent a definitive break from classical sovereignty but instead entails the extension and generalization of the state of exception that founds sovereign power. Hence Agamben argues that the biopolitical regime of power operative in modernity is not so much distinguished by incorporating life into politics, as Foucault claimed, but by the fact that the "state of exception comes more and more to the foreground as the fundamental political structure and ultimately begins to become the rule" (*HS*: 20). Or, again, "together with the process by which the exception everywhere becomes the rule, the realm of bare life – which is originally situated at the margins of the political order – gradually begins to coincide with the political realm, and exclusion and inclusion, outside and inside, *bios* and *zoē*, right and fact, enter into a zone of irreducible indistinction" (*ibid.*: 9).

The theoretical point of inspiration for this claim comes from the eighth fragment of Benjamin's "Theses on the Philosophy of History", where he writes:

> The tradition of the oppressed teaches us that the "state of emergency" in which we live is not the exception but the rule. We must attain to a conception of history that accords with this insight. Then we will clearly see that it is our task to bring about a real state of emergency, and this will improve our position in the struggle against fascism.[14]

Taking up the first theoretical provocation in this thesis, Agamben generalizes the sovereign exception such that it no longer appears as the exceptional case, but as the norm. This means that the capture of bare life within the exception is a general condition of existence, such that the rule and the exception, inclusion and exclusion, and right and violence are no longer clearly distinguishable. Agamben claims from this that under a regime of biopolitics all subjects are each potentially *homo sacer* (*HS*: 115). That is, all subjects are at least potentially if not actually abandoned by the law and exposed to violence as a constitutive condition of political existence. As empirical evidence of this politico-philosophical claim, he cites the Roman legal figure of *homo sacer*, genocidal violence, the apparently ever-expanding phenomenon of concentration camps – which he argues reveal the "nomos of the modern" – as well as the redefinition of life and death in the categories of the "overcomatose" or brain-dead, and neo-morts. Perhaps unsurprisingly, Agamben has been heavily criticized for his apparently eclectic collection of empirical evidence and the rendering of these examples as "indistinguishable". Yet what unites the examples Agamben uses is the thesis on the generalization of the exception and the correlative indistinction of fact and norm in Western politics and philosophy.

I shall say more about the methodological implications of the generalization of the exception in terms of an analysis of contemporary juridico-political conditions in Chapter 4. But first I want to continue the discussion of the theoretical or conceptual implications of this point. What is crucial about Agamben's recourse to both Schmitt's thesis on the exception and Benjamin's more radical version of it is that it means that Agamben places the exception at the heart of contemporary juridico-politics. Contemporary politics is thus a version of exceptional politics, in which the rule of law operates in suspension. But while Agamben appears sympathetic to the Schmittian version of exceptional politics in *Homo Sacer*, there is a subtle shift in his position in the companion text, *State of Exception*. Cast as a genealogy of the theory of the exception, this book posits that "the state of exception tends increasingly to appear as the dominant paradigm of government in contemporary politics" (*SE*: 2). From this perspective, the interest of Schmitt's theory of the exception is that it complicates the simple *topographical* articulation of the exception – as entailing a clear distinction between norm/exception, inside/outside or law/lawlessness, for instance – into a more complex *topological* relation in which what is at issue is "the very limit of the juridical order" (*ibid.*: 23). But while indicating the importance of Schmitt, Agamben's ultimate sympathy with Benjamin becomes clearer throughout this text. Ultimately, Agamben's case will be that while Schmitt harnesses the power of the exception back to the juridical order, Benjamin releases that power into a new politics beyond law and beyond the state.

State of Exception clarifies and extends the onto-political characterization of sovereignty, law and legal violence that Agamben initially elaborates in *Homo Sacer*. In the earlier text, he describes the modern condition of law as one of "being in force without significance", a condition that is effectively equivalent to abandonment, wherein the subject of law is wholly given over to the violence of law and simultaneously bereft of its protection. This condition emerges from the fact that the state of exception that founds sovereignty has become the rule, such that the law is suspended and yet remains in force. The later text elaborates on this thesis, again beginning with the claim of an essential contiguity between the state of exception and sovereignty posited by Carl Schmitt in *Political Theology*. For Agamben, the general employment by law of the state of exception that this entails is the condition by which law simultaneously appropriates and abandons life. Within this, the unfounded decision of the sovereign is the "threshold", since it is in the decision that the originary non-coincidence between life and law is breached and life is truly brought into the sphere of law.

To make this argument, Agamben begins with an analysis of the state of exception in Schmitt's work. He argues that the theory of sovereignty that he proposes in *Political Theology* – captured in the dictum that "sovereign is he who decides on the exception" – is based upon the prior theorization in *Dictatorship*; both amount to an attempt to inscribe the exception within law. In this, Schmitt establishes the topology of the exception as "being-outside yet belonging", and because the sovereign is defined by the exception, it can also be defined by the "oxymoron ecstasy–belonging", where "ecstasy" should be understood in its full resonance of being outside or beside oneself. In the course of these two studies, Schmitt establishes in the body of law a number of "caesuras and divisions", which by virtue of their opposition and articulation allow the law to operate at all. The most interesting of these oppositions here is that between the law and its application, from which Agamben concludes, "the state of exception separates the norm from its application in order to make its application possible. It introduces a zone of anomie into the law in order to make the effective regulation [*normazione*] of the real possible" (*SE*: 36).

The separation of law and its force in application leads Agamben to posit the notion of "force-of-~~law~~" to describe a situation in which the force of law is not tied to law *per se*, but is instead an indeterminate element: it describes the "force of law without law". This idea of "force-of-~~law~~" makes apparent a homologue between law and language, in so far as both contain indeterminate elements that only take on significance in their appropriation or application. From this homologue, Agamben concludes that:

> just as between language and the world, so between the norm and its application there is no internal nexus that allows one to be derived immediately from the other . . . the state of exception is the opening of a space in which application and norm reveal their separation and a pure force-of-~~law~~ realizes . . . a norm whose application has been suspended . . . in order to apply a norm it is ultimately necessary to suspend its application, to produce an exception. (*SE*: 40)

This gives a clearer indication of the phrase "law in force without significance" that Agamben had introduced in *Homo Sacer*, and in doing so, indicates the fundamental location of the exception within the operation of the normal politico-juridical sphere. That is, while the law can only apply in normal situations, as Schmitt posits, its application is nevertheless conditional upon its suspension through the production of an exception.

At this point, Agamben's thought seems well contained within the Schmittian framework, a characteristic for which he has been criticized on more than one occasion. But he is not satisfied to rest here, for after having established the exceptional structure of contemporary politics, Agamben now radicalizes the exception in order to find that *euporic* resolution of the *aporias* of contemporary democracy that he argues any kind of genuinely political thought must confront. Thus, in the chapter entitled "Gigantomachy concerning a Void", he argues that the characterization of the state of exception developed by Schmitt is in fact nothing other than a response to Benjamin's affirmation in "Critique of Violence"[15] of a wholly anomic sphere of human action captured in the notion of a divine or pure violence. Schmitt attempts, Agamben argues, to harness this sphere again to the operation of law by making it the topological condition of law's operation in suspension. Against this, Agamben affirms the importance of the distinction between the virtual and real state of exception posited by Benjamin in his eighth thesis on the philosophy of history, which provides the means by which Benjamin can disable or thwart Schmitt's recuperative move.

Suggesting that the eighth thesis on the philosophy of history is the most decisive document in the dossier of the Benjamin–Schmitt engagement, Agamben argues that the indeterminacy of the norm and exception posited in the eighth thesis (where "the exception has become the rule") is intolerable for Schmitt. It means that the sovereign decision would be effectively undermined, devoured by that off which it lives. Thus what is at stake in the Benjamin–Schmitt debate is the juridical apparatus founded on the exception understood as an anomic space, in which, Agamben suggests, the relation between law and violence comes to the fore. What is significant about the eighth thesis, then, is not only the claim of the exception becoming the rule, but also the exhortation to bring about a real state of exception. For Benjamin, the real state of exception is the anomic sphere of pure violence, of human action released from law and the instrumental violence this entails (SE: 52–64). As such, the purity of divine violence does not indicate some particular quality or inherent characteristic of that violence, but indicates that divine violence supersedes the means–end relation of instrumentality such that it "holds itself in relation to its own mediality" (*ibid.*: 62). This means that the purity of divine violence refers to its decoupling from an end outside itself and thus the attainment of pure mediality or status as pure means. At this point, we are coming up against the politics of pure means that Agamben develops from Benjamin. But rather than take up this issue here, it is first worth returning to the notion of bare life that Agamben relies on in the *Homo Sacer* project. This will later allow a fuller articulation of the politics of pure means.

The elusive figure of "bare life"

Agamben's conception of bare or naked life ("*nuda vita*") has perhaps been one of the most productive for those wanting to use his work as a diagnostics of contemporary political conditions. For instance, it has been used as a tool for understanding phenomena as diverse as the international legal status of refugees, suicide bombers, and the social status of poverty-stricken HIV sufferers of Brazil among others. Agamben has also contributed to extending the apparent empirical reach of the concept in his references to the case of Karen Quinlan, the notion of the "overcomatose" proposed in France, the systematic use of rape as a weapon of war, and the history of self-experimentation in science.[16] Yet it is not clear that the notion of bare life can be extracted from the extensive critique of the history of metaphysics in the way that its use as a diagnostics often presupposes it can be. If it cannot be so easily extracted from this critique, then a more substantial philosophical apparatus is at stake in uses of this notion than is usually acknowledged. This raises a question about its real value as a diagnostic tool that is usually left implicit. Additionally, in part because of this failure, the notion of "bare life" has given rise to a great deal of misunderstanding in literature on *Homo Sacer*, as it is frequently conflated with natural, nutritive life. No doubt this is in part the consequence of a degree of conceptual confusion and slippage on Agamben's part, such that it often appears that he uses the term "bare life" to also refer to natural life.

This confusion or slippage could be attributed to the fact that various forms of life are themselves blurred in contemporary democracy.[17] But if bare life is simply understood as synonymous with nutritive life, Agamben's rejection of the thesis on sacrifice and the sacralization of life and his frequent gesture to a new "form-of-life" become increasingly opaque. The equation of bare life with natural life would render his thesis on the sovereign exception trivial at best and nonsensical at worst. What has to be kept in mind is that it is precisely the exposure to (non-sacrificial) violence that marks bare life as both inside and outside the political order, as the "zone of indistinction" or excrescence produced in the division of biological life and political life. The new "form-of-life" that Agamben goes on to posit thus aims to overcome the exposure of bare life to biosovereign violence through rendering impossible the division of nutritive and political life. There are thus four categories of life that operate in *Homo Sacer* and throughout other texts: *zoē* or biological life, *bios* or political life, bare life (sometimes rendered as sacred life or naked life, from the original Italian term "*nuda vita*") and a new "form-of-life", occasionally rendered as "happy life". In this section, I outline the various notions of "life" that Agamben uses and the role they play in his political theory. This will help us see more clearly what is at stake in Agamben's reformulation of politics as "means without end", which I discuss in the final chapter. It will also allow Agamben's work to be situated alongside that of contemporaries such as Antonio Negri, who uses the term "biopolitics" in recent work but in a manner that is at odds with Agamben's conception.

Noting the etymology of the word "life", Agamben highlights that the Ancient Greeks had two semantically distinct terms for it: "*zoē*, which expressed the simple fact of living common to all living beings (animals, men or gods), and *bios*, which indicated the form or way of living proper to an individual or a group" (*HS*: 1). With this distinction in mind, Foucault's conception of biopolitics signals the entry not of "life" in its generality into politics, but rather the integration of what is captured by the more specific designation of *zoē* or natural life. What is at stake in modern politics according to Foucault is the simple living body of the individual and the species. As Agamben states, for Foucault "the entry of *zoē* into the sphere of the polis . . . constitutes the decisive event of modernity and signals a radical transformation of the political–philosophical categories of political thought" (*ibid*.: 4). As we have seen, the revision of Agamben's thesis in relation to Foucault revolves around the claim that natural life has *always* been included in politics – even if only through its exclusion. But while Agamben moves away from Foucault's more historically and empirically restrained theses on the emergence and institutionalization of biopower, this does not mean that he sees no substantive difference between classical and modern democracy.

Rather, Agamben suggests that what distinguishes modern democracy from classical democracy is that the former "presents itself from the beginning as a vindication and liberation of *zoē*, and that it is constantly trying to transform its own bare life into a way of life and to find, so to speak, the *bios* of *zoē*" (*HS*: 10). That is, the *raison d'être* of contemporary political power is the annulment of the distinction between *bios* and *zoē* – it aims towards a total politicization of biological life that undercuts the distinction between *bios* and *zoē* and therefore eradicates bare life. At the same time though, Agamben claims, modern democracy consistently fails in the endeavour to reconcile *bios* and *zoē*, such that "bare life remains included in politics in the form of the exception, that is, as something which is included solely through an exclusion" (*ibid*.: 11). While modern politics is increasingly played out on the level of biological life, in its attempt to discover the *bios* of *zoē* it nevertheless continually produces bare life as the excrescence of its failure, thereby preventing the overcoming of the sovereign exception and the violence that conditions bare life. This situation leads to an *aporia* specific to modern democracy: "it wants to put the freedom and happiness of men into play in the very place – 'bare life' – that marked their subjection" (*ibid.*: 10). This *aporia* persists because modern politics has been unable to "heal the fracture" between *bios* and *zoē*, and until an adequate response is at hand, politics will continue to play out on the terrain of violence and death.

The problem that contemporary thought must face, then, is not only to discover the originary relation that underpins and gives rise to this *aporia*, but also to find a way to think beyond it. The task for Agamben is to transform this *aporia* into a *euporia* – to transform the lack of a way into a felicitous way or path (WP: 217). Understanding the originary relation of life and sovereignty is only the first step, though it is a necessary one. And as the title *Homo Sacer* suggests, one of the keys to understanding and overcoming this *aporia* is a clarification of the politico-theological thesis that proclaims a sacredness internal to life itself.

In his essay, "Critique of Violence", Benjamin suggests that one of the key questions that contemporary thought must confront in order to move beyond legal or mythic violence is that of the origin of the "dogma" of the sacredness of life.[18] Responding to Benjamin's provocation, Agamben argues that the sacredness of life emerges only to the extent that life is incorporated into the sovereign exception: "life is sacred only insofar as it is taken into the sovereign exception" (*HS*: 85). Consequently, he rejects recourse to the notion of the sacredness of life against the power of the sovereign in the form of power over life and death, and claims instead that it is precisely the sacralization of life that permits it capture within the sovereign exception, and the concomitant production of bare life. As he states, the "sacredness of life, which is invoked today as an absolutely fundamental right in opposition to sovereign power, in fact originally expresses precisely both life's subjection to a power over death and life's irreparable exposure in the relation of abandonment" (*ibid.*: 83).

To outline this thesis further, Agamben invokes the figure of "sacred man" or *homo sacer* from Roman law. In particular, he takes up the definition of sacred man given by Pompius Festus, who writes that "the sacred man is the one whom the people have judged on account of a crime. It is not permitted to sacrifice this man, yet he who kills him will not be condemned for homicide" (cited in *HS*: 71). Agamben claims that the apparently contradictory traits of the sacred man, which allow that he can be killed with impunity but not according to ritual practices, have so far eluded full explanation. Agamben rejects explanation of these characteristics through positing an essential ambiguity of the sacred on the basis of circularity, and argues instead that the sacred man is most properly understood to be characterized by a "double exclusion and a double capture" (*HS*: 82). That sacred man can be killed but is unable to be sacrificed means that this figure is set outside the purview of human law and is simultaneously excluded from divine law, since to be sacrificed is to be given over to the gods, dedicated to or revered as if of the gods, a fate from which sacred man is excluded. Consequently, the violence committed against *homo sacer* does not constitute sacrilege but is instead considered licit (*ibid.*). Agamben goes on to argue that the double exclusion of sacred man points to a correlative double inclusion in the realms of the divine and the human, since the formal characteristics of being able to be killed and not sacrificed also indicate inclusion of *homo sacer* within the human community and his belonging to God. He states that "*homo sacer* belongs to God in the form of unsacrificeability and is included in the community in the form of being able to be killed" (*ibid.*). He concludes from this contradictory status that sacred or bare life is life lived beyond both divine and profane law, and is thus life singularly exposed to death.

However, the "double exclusion and double capture" of bare life means that the zone in which bare life persists is not simply lawless, but instead reveals the inclusive exclusion or abandonment of bare life *vis-à-vis* law. Furthermore, it reveals a fundamental homology between *homo sacer* and the exception, in that each is simultaneously included and excluded from the law and thus subject to the sovereign decision (*HS*: 84). For Agamben, the figure of *homo sacer* expresses the originary political relation, as this figure recalls the memory of the exclusions that found the juridico-political sphere as the excrescence of the religious and profane, and illuminates the indistinction between sacrificial and homicidal violence that lies at the heart of sovereign power. Hence he states that "the sovereign sphere is the sphere in which it is permitted to kill without committing homicide and without celebrating a sacrifice, and sacred life – that is life that may be killed but not sacrificed – is the life that has been captured in this sphere" (*ibid.*: 83). A symmetry then becomes apparent between *homo sacer* and sovereignty, for while "the sovereign is the one with respect to whom all men are potentially *homines sacri* . . . *homo sacer* is the one with respect to whom all men act as sovereign" (*ibid.*: 84). But to add an important caveat, Agamben does not see the proximity of sacredness and sovereignty as the "secularized residue of the originary religious character of every political power" (*ibid.*: 84–5), or as an attempt to provide a theological foundation for politics. Rather, sacredness constitutes the "originary" form of the inclusion of bare life in the juridical order, and the syntagm *homo sacer* brings to light the inclusive exclusion of bare life in the political order as the object of the sovereign decision, and thus names the "originary political relation".

If this sheds light on the originary form of the *aporia* of modern democracy, it also means that recourse to a notion of the sacredness of life cannot provide grounds for opposition to biopolitical sovereignty, since the invocation of this relation will endlessly repeat the *aporia* without breaking free of it. But while Agamben rejects attempts to rescue life from its entrapment in sovereign power through sacralization, he also rejects notions of a force of opposition or resistance in biological life itself. This should make clear his distance from theorists working in the tradition of Spinoza, Bergson and vitalistic approaches to the concept of life. One philosopher working in this tradition whose work Agamben has commented on is Gilles Deleuze; interestingly, though, Agamben appears less critical of his conception of "a life" as "absolute immanence" than might be expected. In an essay that resists at least as much as it achieves clarification of the concept of life,[19] Agamben comments on Deleuze's final published work, in which he develops a conception of a non-subjective or "impersonal" life composed of "virtualities, events, singularities"[20] that may be manifest in but are not reducible to an individual. Emphasizing Deleuze's reference to "beautitude" and the "pure bliss" of a life as absolute immanence, Agamben concludes that "the element that marks subjection to biopower" must be discerned "in the very paradigm of possible beatitude" such that "blessed life lies on the same terrain as the biological body of the West" (AI: 238–9). On the one hand, this comment appears to align a conception of blessed life with the nutritive life of the body that Agamben sees as central to the operation of biopolitical subjection. But on the other hand, Agamben argues that Deleuze's conception of life as absolute immanence can be understood as "pure contemplation beyond every subject and object of knowledge; it is pure potentiality that preserves without acting" (*ibid*.: 234). This latter formulation runs close to Agamben's own formulation of potentiality as the indeterminacy between possibility and actuality, or between the (self-) preservation of pure power that exists without passing into action. In this, Agamben seems both close to and far from Deleuze's interpretation of the concept of life.

Perhaps some of the ambiguity of Agamben's formulation can be explained by the fact that while Deleuze's formulation of an impersonal life refers to something akin to a non-biologistic vital principle or force, Agamben's point of reference is the distinction between biological or nutritive life and ways of life articulated by Aristotle. That is, whereas for Deleuze the pure power of absolute immanence of an impersonal life is best articulated in relation to Bergson and the creative force within life itself, for Agamben the point of interest is the suspensive indeterminacy between one state or another. Accordingly, in their respective interpretations of the Charles Dickens story of Riderhood, the rogue that wavers on the point of living and dying, they each emphasize quite different points of interpretation. Whereas Deleuze sees in Riderhood's predicament the power of something soft and sweet that penetrates[21] but which is separable from the individual in which it is manifest, Agamben emphasizes the point of indeterminacy between life and death, which he describes as a "happy netherworld" which is "neither in this world nor in the next, but between the two" and which one "seems to leave only reluctantly".[22] Hence, while Deleuze's references to "*homo tantum*" and beatitude (understood as a profane blissful happiness) seem on the face of it to be close to Agamben's conceptions of "*nuda vita*" and "*vita beata*", closer inspection shows them to be approaching these ideas from very different perspectives. Deleuze from the vitalist position of pure creative force; Agamben from a revised Aristotelianism that emphasizes a topological indeterminacy that is homologous with that of the state of exception.

Agamben's emphasis on topological indeterminacy has significant consequences for understanding his theory of politics and political resistance: it underpins his formulation of preserving without acting that will be central to his notion of a "politics of pure means" that he derives from Benjamin. But for now, it is worth noting that this points to the deep theoretical rift between Agamben and other Italian political theorists such as Antonio Negri, who argues against the separation of potentiality and acting that Agamben emphasizes. Instead, Negri emphasizes the creative, "constituent power" of the life of a multiplicity in action in opposition to the sovereign state form. In his book *Insurgencies*, Negri addresses the distinction between constituting and constituted power (where the former can be understood pre-theoretically as the power of creation and the latter as the institutionalized force that is created) to argue that constituting or "constituent" power cannot be equated with sovereignty.

This is because, while constituent power is a free act of creation that is not exhausted in what is created, sovereignty limits and fixes constituent power. Negri writes

> the truth of constituent power is not what can be attributed to it, in any way whatsoever, by the concept of sovereignty . . . [constituent power] is, rather, an act of choice, the precise determination that opens a horizon, the radical apparatus of something that does not yet exist, and whose conditions of existence imply that the creative act does not lose its characteristics in the act of creating. When constituent power sets in motion the constituent process, every determination is free and remains free. On the contrary, sovereignty presents itself as a fixing of constituent power, and therefore as its termination, as the exhaustion of the freedom that constituent power carries.[23]

For Negri, constituent power is the power of the multitude, which is the true political subject such that the political is by definition "the ontological strength of a multitude of cooperating singularities".[24] Moreover, the multitude is life, which is continuously subjected to the subtraction of its power (*potenza*) of creation by a "power of the nothing", such as state domination and capitalist exploitation.[25] According to Negri and his long-time collaborator, Michael Hardt, Agamben's error is to construe bare or naked life as fundamentally passive in relation to sovereign violence, singularly exposed without recourse or response. By contrast, Negri and Hardt claim in *Empire* that Nazism and fascism do not reveal the essential passivity of bare life so much as amount to an attempt to destroy "the enormous power that naked life could become".[26] For them, Agamben's understanding of naked or bare life merely exposes "behind the political abysses that modern totalitarianism has constructed the (more or less) heroic conditions of passivity" separated from action.[27]

In contrast, in *Homo Sacer*, Agamben rejects Negri's attempt to separate constituent power from sovereignty, and instead equates potentiality with sovereignty. This equation is indicated in his characterization of a "matchless potentiality" of the *nomos* and explicitly posited in his discussion of Aristotle's conception of potentiality. In this, Agamben claims that the paradox of sovereignty is most clearly evident in the distinction between constituting and constituted power, where constituting power is essentially identical with sovereign power in so far as each is concerned with the "constitution of potentiality".[28] That is, sovereign power is essentially co-equal to constituent power in that neither can be determined by the existing order and nor can either be limited to constituting that order but are instead "free praxis" and potentiality.[29]

Explicitly politicizing the problem of potentiality, Agamben claims that Aristotle "actually bequeathed the paradigm of sovereignty to Western philosophy. For the sovereign ban, which applies to the exception in no longer applying, corresponds to the structure of potentiality, which maintains itself in relation to actuality precisely through its ability not to be" (*HS*: 46). Agamben argues that the structure of potentiality corresponds to that of the operation of the sovereign, wherein the sovereign decides on what the law applies to. He claims that potentiality is "that through which Being founds itself *sovereignly* . . . without anything preceding or determining it . . . other than its own ability not to be. And an act is sovereign when it realizes itself by simply taking away its own potentiality not to be, letting itself be, giving itself to itself" (*ibid.*). Moreover, the particular force of the sovereign in relation to the exception is that it maintains itself indefinitely in its own potentiality, that is, its own not passing into actuality through the structure of not applying, of withdrawing from the exception. This means that the problem of sovereignty returns political philosophy to ontology, which necessitates a rethinking of the metaphysical relation between potentiality and actuality (as discussed in Chapter 1). While Negri concurs that politics entails rethinking political ontology, the point of their disagreement is the designation of potentiality as on the side of the sovereign or on the side of life or the "multitude".

This also helps to make sense of Agamben's rejection of Foucault's formulation of a political response to biopolitics at the end of *The History of Sexuality*, where he calls for the inauguration of a new "economy of bodies and pleasures" to combat biopolitical subjection and the deployment of sexuality. In this formulation at least, Foucault appears to claim that natural, biological life might be the site of resistance to biopolitical subjection.[30] This interpretation of Foucault is given further strength by his suggestion that life has not been totally integrated into the techniques that govern it but constantly escapes them, as well as his claim that struggles against biopolitics "relied for support on the very thing [power] invested, that is, on life and man as a living being".[31] The theoretical underpinning of this claim is that resistance is never external to power, but is inscribed in relations of power as the "irreducible opposite", the "odd term" that provides the "adversary, target, support or handle" for their strategic operation.[32] Resistance is an immanent possibility within any confrontation of power relations, and it is precisely that which power targets that provides the points of opposition, resistance and possible transformation. Foucault locates the possibility of escaping the capture of biopolitical techniques within the forces of the body itself, and resistance is enacted through the immanent potential for reversal within relations of power.

But according to Agamben, the aporetic violence of modern democracy stymies any attempt to oppose biopolitical regimes from within the framework of *bios* and *zoē*. Such projects will tirelessly repeat the *aporia* of the exception, the danger of which lies in the gradual convergence of democracy with totalitarianism. In other words, the condition of abandonment indicates a fundamental *aporia* for contemporary politics, where attempts to overcome the capture of life within the sovereign exception through recourse to natural life necessarily repeat and reinstall that capture in their politicization of natural life. Thus Agamben rejects Foucault's gesture towards a new economy of bodies and their pleasures, claiming that the "'body' is always already a biopolitical body and bare life, and nothing in it or the economy of its pleasure seems to allow us to find solid ground on which to oppose the demands of sovereign power" (*HS*: 187).

The implication of this for a theory of political resistance is that Agamben must locate the possibility for resistance outside the triad of *bios*, *zoē* and bare life, and in doing so, he urges a radical rethinking of both life and politics. As he writes,

> Until a completely new politics – that is, a politics no longer founded on the *exceptio* of bare life – is at hand, every theory and every praxis will remain imprisoned and immobile, and the "beautiful day" of life will be given citizenship only either through blood and death or in the perfect senselessness to which the society of the spectacle condemns it.
>
> (*Ibid.*: 11)

The only means of escape from contemporary biopolitics is through a reconsideration of the notion of life apart from the separation of bare life from political life, such that a "coming politics" that no longer takes bare life as its ground is made possible.

In this light, it becomes evident that Agamben's theorization of a "form-of-life" or "happy life" plays an important role in his political theory, namely, to point towards a way of overcoming the sovereign ban by reconciling the distinction between *bios* and *zoē*. As he writes in *Means without End*,

> The "happy life" on which political philosophy should be founded thus cannot be either the naked life that sovereignty posits as a presupposition so as to turn it into its own subject or the impenetrable extraneity of science and of modern biopolitics that everybody today tries in vain to sacralize. This "happy life" should be, rather, an absolutely profane "sufficient life" that has reached the perfection of its own power and of its own communicability – a life over which sovereignty and right no longer have any hold.
>
> (*ME*: 114–15)

Agamben's new conception of life, described as "happy life" or a "form-of-life", allows no separation between *bios* and *zoē*. Instead, it is unified in an absolute immanence to itself, in "the perfection of its own power". He seeks nothing short of a politico-philosophical redefinition of a life that is no longer founded upon the bloody separation of natural life and political life, and which is in fact beyond every form of relation in so far as it is life lived in pure immanence, grounded on itself alone. The inauguration of happy life in which neither *zoē* nor *bios* can be isolated allows for the law in force without significance to be overcome such that the Nothing maintained by that law is eliminated and humanity reaches its own fulfilment in its immediate transparency to itself. Happy life can be characterized as life lived in the experience of its own unity, its own potentiality of "being-thus" (*CC*: 93),[33] and as such, is life lived beyond the reach of the law (*ME*: 114–15). In this way, Agamben offers a redemptive hope that is external to the problems of biopolitics; the problems posed by the state of exception and sovereignty's capture of bare life are resolved by the inauguration of happy life, and the coming politics it grounds redeems humanity in the face of biopolitical capture and annihilation. This requires rethinking the very nature of politics, along with the life that is captured within the sovereign ban.

One of the central gestures leading to this conception of happy life is the emphasis on topological indeterminacy, which plays an important role in Agamben's formulation of a politics of pure means. In "Critique of Violence" and elsewhere, Benjamin proposes that what is required is a formulation of politics that is no longer tied to instrumental reason and, as such, exceeds the conceptual linkage of means and ends. While Agamben does not explicitly adopt the figuration of divine violence outlined by Benjamin, the quest for a politics of "pure means" or "means without end" is central to his political philosophy. For Agamben, such a politics is possible only outside the division and nexus of biological and political life, and must be founded on the notion of happy life or "form-of-life". As I discuss in the following chapters, a politics of pure means is directly related to Agamben's conception of potentiality, and the perceived necessity of a pure language – of returning to communicability as such without reference to language as a tool or means to achieve the end of communication.

I shall say more of Agamben's "coming politics" in the chapter on messianism; for now, it is worth noting that this conception of politics is also deeply integrated with the Hegelian and post-Hegelian thesis on the end of history. However, Agamben wishes to push further all previous formulations of the end of history, by arguing that the coming politics not only requires the end of history, but also the simultaneous end of the state. He argues that contemporary thought furnishes a number of examples of a desire for one or the other of these, but neither of these approaches is adequate to the task of the "coming thought" since "to think the extinction of the state without the fulfilment of the historical telos is as impossible as to think a fulfilment of history in which the empty form of state sovereignty would continue to exist". The first of these approaches is "impotent against the tenacious survival of the state-form" while the second "clashes against the increasingly powerful resistance of historical instances (of a national, religious, or ethnic type)" (*ME*: 111).

Heidegger's notion of *Ereignis* is for Agamben one attempt to grasp the end of history and the end of the state simultaneously, although it is "an entirely unsatisfactory" one. *Ereignis* is here understood to indicate an event of an unprecedented, unrepeatable order which seizes or appropriates from historical destiny "the being-hidden itself of the historical principle, that is, historicity itself" (*ibid.*: 111). This requires that human beings take possession of their own nature as historical beings; that is, of their own "impropriety" (which for Agamben is most clearly manifest in language) and make it their most proper nature. At this point, then, we can begin to see the interconnection between Agamben's critique of biopower and sovereignty, and formulation of "form-of-life" as the ground of a coming politics, his early formulation of infancy, and the conception of history and temporality that he proposes. This interconnection will be explored more fully in the later chapter on messianism. For now, we can simply state that this means that the utilization of the notion of bare life as a diagnostic tool entails the adoption of an intricate conceptual apparatus that is rarely examined in such uses. The question that has to be asked, then, is whether this conceptual apparatus really synchronizes with the political, social and ethical aims of critical uses of the notion of bare life. Can Agamben's conception of a politics beyond history and beyond the state support the critical interventions into contemporary socio-political and juridical conditions that seem to motivate many uses of the notion of "bare life"? This is the question that will be pursued over the next two chapters.

CHAPTER FOUR

Ethics: testimony, responsibility and the witness

The wish of all, in the camps, the last wish: know what has happened, do not forget, and at the same time never will you know.
(Blanchot, *The Writing of the Disaster*, 82)

As we saw in Chapter 3, Agamben appropriates Walter Benjamin's apothegm that the exception has become the rule as a means of responding to the Schmittian conception of sovereignty and law as founded on the exception. Solidifying this thesis through empirical reference, Agamben subsequently argues that the paradigmatic manifestation of exceptional biopolitics is the concentration camp. Given this critique of the camps and the status of the law that is revealed in them, it is no surprise that Agamben takes the most extreme manifestation of the condition of the camps as a starting point for an elaboration of an ethics without reference to the law, a term that is taken to encompass normative discourse in its entirety. In *Remnants of Auschwitz*, published as the third volume of the Homo Sacer series, Agamben develops an account of an ethics of testimony as an ethos of bearing witness to that for which one cannot bear witness. Taking up the problem of scepticism in relation to the Nazi concentration camps of World War II – also discussed by Jean-François Lyotard and others – Agamben casts *Remnants* as an attempt to listen to a lacuna in survivor testimony, in which the factual condition of the camps cannot be made to coincide with what is said about them. However, Agamben is not concerned with the epistemological issues that this non-coincidence of "fact and truth" raises but, rather, with the ethical implications with which, he suggests, our age has so far failed to reckon.

The key figure in his account of an ethics of testimony is that of the *Muselmänner* (the Muslims), or those in the camps who had reached such a state of physical decrepitude and existential disregard that "one hesitates to call them living: one hesitates to call their death death".[1] But rather than seeing the *Muselmann* as the limit-figure between life and death, Agamben argues that the *Muselmann* is more correctly understood as the limit-figure of the human and inhuman. As the threshold between the human and the inhuman, the *Muselmann* does not simply mark the limit beyond which the human is no longer human. Agamben argues that such a stance would merely repeat the experiment of Auschwitz, in which the *Muselmann* is put outside the limits of the human and the moral status that attends that categorization. Instead, the *Muselmann* indicates a more fundamental lack of distinction between the human and the inhuman, in which it is impossible definitively to separate one from the other, and which calls into question the moral distinctions that rest on this designation. The key question that arises for Agamben, then, is whether there is a "humanity to the human" over and above biologically belonging to the species, and it is in reflecting on this question that Agamben develops his account of ethics. In doing so, he rejects recourse to standard moral concepts such as dignity and respect, claiming that "Auschwitz marks the end and the ruin of every ethics of dignity and conformity to a norm . . . The Muselmann . . . is the guard on the threshold of a new ethics, an ethics of a form of life that begins where dignity ends" (*RA*: 69).

In providing "signposts" for navigating this new ethical terrain, Agamben returns to the definition of the human as the being who has language to bring out a double movement in the human subject's appropriation of language. In particular, the analysis of pronouns discussed in earlier chapters, in which pronouns allow a speaker to put language to use, is central to the analysis of ethical subjectivity that Agamben develops in *Remnants*. Agamben argues that the appropriation of language in speaking reveals both a process of subjectification (or becoming subject) and a simultaneous and inevitable desubjectification. That is, because pronouns are simply grammatical shifters or "indicators of enunciation" that refer only to the taking place of language itself, the appropriation of language in the identification of oneself as a speaking subject requires that the psychosomatic individual simultaneously erase or desubjectify itself. This also makes evident the unspoken in speech, which is not – as we learned from *Language and Death* – a radical unspeakability, but an infantile muteness that provides the very condition of communicability.

As this suggests, the account of an ethics of "non-responsibility" in *Remnants* bridges Agamben's analysis of language and the later analysis of the camps as the paradigm of modern politics. In this chapter, I primarily elaborate the form of a non-juridical ethics that Agamben develops on the basis of his linguistic and political analysis. But I also begin to develop two angles of critique of Agamben's work to this point: first, I discuss his ethical and political philosophy in relation to more standard normative concepts such as rights and justice. Secondly, I discuss the non-relational and highly dematerialized conception of ethical subjectivity that he develops. These negative points of critique lead into an extended discussion of the positive conception of politics, history and happiness that Agamben offers under the rubric of a "politics of pure means" in Chapter 5. To begin, though, I return to Agamben's treatment of the camps and the methodological implications of adopting the apothegm that the exception has become the rule.

The camp as paradigm

In his sociological study of the relation of the Holocaust to modernity, Zygmunt Bauman argues that there is a much tighter integration than is usually recognized between the social-structural characteristics of modernity and the genocide that took place during World War II.[2] Bauman argues against typical sociological approaches that emphasize psychosocial factors and make the Holocaust appear as an anomalous event with little in common with structural elements of modernity, and claims instead that the Holocaust is of a piece with the instrumental rationality characteristic of bureaucratic modernity. In his Weberian analysis, the characteristics of bureaucratic reason made the Holocaust possible: the physical extermination of Jews was simply a technical solution to the problem of attaining a "Jew-free" Europe and simply the "product of routine bureaucratic procedures" such as instrumental or means–ends rationalization and the universal application of the rule. For Bauman, modernity provides the systemic conditions under which the Holocaust became possible. Given this close association, it is no doubt tempting to see Bauman's argument as a sociological equivalent of the more philosophical–theoretical argument posed by Agamben that the camp has become the "nomos of the modern". In this vein, Nikolas Rose argues against the perceived pessimism of both, to claim that modern biopolitics is less about the production of death than about the maintenance of life.[3]

But while there is a superficial similarity in Bauman and Agamben's characterizations, it would be an error to see them as "fellow-travellers" in any more substantial way. When Bauman's *Modernity and the Holocaust* was published, the critical reception was varied, but rarely took the form of accusations such as Ernesto Laclau's against Agamben, that his thesis is "extreme and absurd".[4] There are of course various external factors that may account for the difference in critical response. But one internal factor that makes their theses incommensurate is simply their characterizations of the relation between the Holocaust and modernity. For Bauman, the Holocaust was a product of bureaucratic rationality and its unchecked application to social organization, but he is explicit that this does not mean that the Holocaust was in any way determined by instrumental reason or an inexorable result of it. For him, while modern civilization was the necessary condition of the Holocaust, it was by no means its sufficient condition.[5] In contrast, for Agamben, the Nazi genocide was indicative of a hidden logic intrinsic to Western politics, and the paroxysms of World War II merely brought this logic to light in an unprecedented way. The camps themselves, though, are nothing other than a paradigmatic expression of this logic.

In extrapolating from Benjamin's claim that the exception has become the rule, Agamben takes the concentration camp as paradigmatic of the logic of the sovereign ban that he diagnoses as the originary relation of Western politics. In this sense, then, the concentration camps of World War II and the "manufacturing of death" that they entailed are inextricably linked with the interrelation of politics and ontology in Western philosophy and, as such, their future prevention requires a radical rethinking of the central concepts of political philosophy – which also extends to rethinking the very nature of "politics" and "philosophy". The conclusion that the fact of the camps requires overcoming a particular way of thinking about politics and philosophy is no doubt jarring to some ears: surely, a retreat to philosophy is not what preventing the recurrence of events such as the Holocaust and other genocides most urgently requires. If nothing else, this could be said to indicate a peculiar and ill-founded belief in the power of philosophical thought to effect sociopolitical transformation on Agamben's part; more specifically, it brings into relief the tight integration of politics and philosophy that Agamben's thought rests on and that also becomes evident in his characterization of the camps as an exercise of modal logic in so far as they impact on the "operators of being" such as potentiality and actuality. I shall return to this characterization of the internal logic of the camps in due course, but first, more needs to be said about the way that the figure of the camp operates within Agamben's analysis.

Agamben maintains that the camps were "born out of the state of exception and martial law" such that the camp is the "materialization of the state of exception" (ME: 38, 41) and the exception is the hidden foundation of Western juridico-political structures as thought from Aristotle onwards. Consequently, the camp is the "hidden matrix" of Western biopolitics, in which these juridico-political structures are most fully revealed. The characterization of the camps as the hidden matrix of Western politics indicates that Agamben sees the camp not simply as the spatialization or materialization of exceptional politics, but as expressing a general logic of contemporary politics. In keeping with the complication of the topography of inside and outside that he suggests is characteristic of the state of exception, Agamben argues that the camp structure mobilized by Nazism is not a simple *topographical* space of confinement. If it were, then the camp could be seen as a technology of confinement in a manner not dissimilar from the way that the prison or hospital operates within Foucault's characterization of disciplinary power. It would remain in keeping with the spatial apparatus of the nation-state that focuses on the control of territory and movement across that territory.

But for Agamben the camp is a *topological* figure. Rather than describing and delimiting a particular locale, the camp reveals an abstract logic that is by no means limited to the geographical space of internment. Hence it is not without significance that Agamben identifies the camp as the *nomos* of the modern, and not only for its reference to Carl Schmitt's study entitled *The Nomos of the Earth*. In *The Human Condition*, Hannah Arendt notes that the etymology of *nomos* links it to territorialization,[6] a spatial metaphorics that is reinforced by the Latin etymology of "exception", which means to take *out-side* (HS: 170). But to the extent that the camp is not merely topographical but topological, then the camp is a "dislocating localization" in which the territorial order of the *nomos* is broken apart by the exception internal to it. Agamben thus writes, "the camp is the fourth and inseparable element that has been added to and has broken up the old trinity of nation (birth), state, and territory" (ME: 44). And to the extent that the figure of the camp expresses a topology of contemporary politics, any more or less innocuous space can be effectively transformed into a camp if the attendant juridico-political structures are brought to bear in that space. Thus he suggests that airport lounges, gated communities, soccer stadiums as much as refugee camps are or can become zones of indeterminacy that are politically and logically equivalent to concentration camps (*ibid.*: 42).

As with the claim that the camp is intrinsic to Western political thought, this extension from the topographic space of the concentration camp to a topological feature of contemporary politics also generates critique of Agamben's thesis. The transformation and proliferation of spaces politically equivalent to the camps that rest on this extension return us to the problem of the proliferation of examples of the logic of the ban and bare life – from the overcomatose to the use of rape in war and self-experimentation in science – in *Homo Sacer* that I mentioned in Chapter 3. Agamben's apparently indiscriminate appropriation of examples for his theoretical claims has come under attack from a number of quarters and often with good reason. However, many of his critics fail to consider the deeper theoretical and methodological commitments guiding the appropriation and use of particular examples to generate a general interpretation. Underpinning this use of examples is a methodological commitment to the notion of the "paradigm", by which Agamben means "an example which defines the intelligibility of the set to which it belongs and at the same time which it constitutes" (WIP). The paradigm allows for the intelligibility of a generality by virtue of the knowability of a singularity, where the generality "does not result from a logic [sic] consequence by means of induction from the exhaustive enumeration of the individual cases". Instead, it entails only the comparison of a singular example "with the object or class that the paradigm will make intelligible" (ibid.).

Interestingly, in articulating this methodology of the paradigm, Agamben likens his approach to that taken by Foucault, who, he argues, always relies on a singular example that will "decide a whole problematic context which it both constitutes and makes intelligible" (WIP).[7] Agamben's primary point of reference to support this likeness is the Panopticon that Foucault analyses as a "diagram of power", the various techniques and strategies of which he encompasses under the name "panopticism" in one chapter of *Discipline and Punish*. Of Jeremy Bentham's plan for the Panopticon as the ideal prison, Foucault writes,

> the Panopticon must not be understood as a dream building: it is the diagram of a mechanism of power reduced to its ideal form; its functioning, abstracted from any obstacle, resistance or friction, must be represented as a pure architectural and optic system: it is in fact a figure of political technology that may and must be detached from any specific use [such that it provides the] general principle of a new "political anatomy" whose object and end are not the relations of sovereignty but the relations of discipline.[8]

But while Foucault's characterization of the Panopticon as the "generalised function" or "general principle" of disciplinary power may seem to lend credence to Agamben's usurpation of Foucault into the "paradigmatic" approach, it should also be kept in mind that Foucault's genealogical method steered away from the search for "originary" relations toward the identification of historically contingent "conditions of emergence".[9]

Moreover, one of the more frequent historiographical criticisms made of Foucault's method is that he tended to overemphasize points of historical breakage and rupture, a tendency that is most clear in his earlier work when he utilizes a historical–epistemological method akin to the approach to scientific paradigms that Agamben draws from Thomas Kuhn. Foucault's early "archaeological" method did attempt to isolate a modern "episteme" through tracing the conditions of possibility of the discursive elements that he called "statements". In this, he is not far from the method of tracing the emergence of concepts used by the French historian of science and medicine, Georges Canguilhem. Further, while in the later genealogical phase figures such as the Panopticon worked as "diagrams" of power relations in a manner not altogether dissimilar to the notion of the paradigm, whereby a singular example both illuminates and constitutes its referent, Foucault also provided extensive analyses of the emergence and transformations of liberal "arts of government", the science of police, discourses of sexuality and psychiatry, and so on. In contrast, Agamben presupposes a temporal continuity on the basis of a "conceptual fundamentalism" in which the origin of a concept determines its subsequent meaning, purpose and valency.[10] In this, his approach stands in sharp contrast to the "tactical polyvalency" of a discourse that Foucault emphasizes in his account of relations of power.[11]

One case in point that reflects this methodological difference is the approach that Foucault and Agamben take to questions of rights. I take up this issue in a later section of this chapter. For now, we can note that, while necessary, recognizing the methodological approach that Agamben takes does not in itself amount to a justification of that approach or a defence against his critics – although it does help to see both the limitations of his approach and of criticisms that fail to take this methodology into account. In my view, regardless of the merit of Agamben's "paradigmatic" approach in itself, it is still the case that he overstretches it. For one, the identification of a figure of Roman law or modern imperial and post-imperial politics as paradigmatic of Western politics from its inception in Aristotle, and which subsequently operates without interruption through the ages, overstretches the notion of a paradigm along with historical credibility. More importantly, the methodological claim that *homo sacer*, or the camp, or the *Muselmänner* are paradigmatic figures of contemporary politics does not in itself justify the logical claim that the danger they represent is intrinsic to Western political thought, nor the claim that this means that the violence of biopolitical sovereignty is an inexorable or unavoidable outcome of that logic. For if history teaches us anything, it may simply be that nothing is inevitable.

Toward an ethics of non-responsibility: subjectivity and language

While Agamben's use of figures such as the camp can and has been disputed, for the sake of further clarification I now set that problem aside and look more closely at the internal logic of the camp as it operates according to Agamben. This will also allow a better view of the importance of the camp for him in terms of a theory of ethics. In *Remnants of Auschwitz*, Agamben takes the condition of the camps as the starting point for a reconsideration of ethics in the light of the biopolitical separation of *bios* and *zoē*, or political life and biological life respectively. In particular, *Remnants* attempts to give philosophical elaboration to the intuitions that guide Primo Levi's essays on the experience of the camps and the ethical status of the survivor as witness. Drawing on Levi's poignant writings, which frequently highlight the ambiguities of survival, judgement and forgiveness, Agamben argues that ethics can no longer be thought through the fundamentally juridical categories of responsibility or dignity. Instead, a new ethics must be sought in a terrain before judgement, in which the conditions of judgement are suspended through the indistinction in the moral categorization of the human and the inhuman.

The privileged figure within Agamben's ethical discourse is that of the *Muselmänner*, who were perhaps the most wretched of the inhabitants of the camp in so far as they were reduced to the status of merely existing – living without purpose, desire or sensation. Locating the figure of the *Muselmann* at the zone of indistinction between the human and the inhuman, Agamben elaborates on "Levi's paradox" that the *Muselmann*, the one who cannot speak, is the true or "complete witness" of the camps.[12] While this paradox raises a number of epistemological questions about the veridical status of experience, Agamben largely sets these aside to focus on the ethical implications of the apparent lacuna between an experience and what can be said about it – that is, between fact and language. In developing his account of ethics, he draws on this lacuna, but focuses more specifically on the collapse of the distinction between the human and inhuman in the biopolitical condition of contemporary politics – which is itself partly a consequence of this lacuna (*RA*: 17). One of the central concerns in this account, then, is whether there is in fact a "humanity of the human" over and above the claim to belong to a biological species that would provide a secure anchorage point for an ethics responsive to the paradoxes presented by the camps and the *Muselmänner*.

To address this, Agamben argues that the *Muselmann* should not be seen as occupying a threshold state between life and death, but is more correctly understood as the limit-figure of the human and inhuman (*RA*: 55). Rather than simply being geared towards the manufacturing of death, then, Auschwitz is the site of an extreme biopolitical experiment, "beyond life and death, in which the Jew is transformed into a *Muselmann* and the human into a non-human" (*ibid.*: 52). However, as the threshold between the human and the inhuman, the figure of the *Muselmann* does not simply mark the limit beyond which the human is no longer human. Agamben argues that such a stance would merely repeat the experiment of Auschwitz that places the *Muselmänner* outside the limits of the human and the moral status that rests on the categorization. Instead, the *Muselmann* indicates a more fundamental indistinction between the human and the inhuman, in which it becomes impossible to distinguish one from the other. The *Muselmann* is an indefinite being in whom (or indeed, in which) the distinction between humanity and non-humanity, as well as the moral categories that attend the distinction, are brought to crisis: Agamben thus describes the *Muselmann* as "the non-human who obstinately appears as human: he is the human that cannot be told apart from the inhuman" (*RA*: 59–69, 82).

Agamben proposes that the human being exists as the nodal point for "currents of the human and inhuman" and states that "human power borders on the inhuman; the human also endures the non-human . . . humans bear within themselves the mark of the inhuman . . . their spirit contains at its very center the wound of non-spirit, non-human chaos atrociously consigned to its own being capable of everything" (*ibid.*: 77). Thus, being human is fundamentally conditioned by an indefinite potentiality for being non-human, for being capable of everything and of enduring the inhuman. Being human is a question of enduring, of "bearing all that one could bear", and surviving the inhuman capacity to bear everything. Importantly, the endurance that remaining human requires takes the form of testimony. Testimony plays a constitutive role in the circulation of the human and inhuman, since remaining human is ultimately a question of bearing witness to the inhuman: "human beings are human insofar as they bear witness to the inhuman" (*ibid.*: 121). In short, to endure the inhuman is to bear witness to it. It is in this sense that Levi speaks of the *Muselmänner* as the true witnesses, for they have endured the inhuman, borne more than they should ever have had to bear, and in doing so, remained fundamentally human. Correlatively, survivors are human to the extent that they bear witness to an impossibility of bearing witness, that is, of being inhuman. Hence testimony arises in the non-coincidental currents of the human and the inhuman, as the human being's bearing witness to the inhuman.

One implication of this is that the ethics of witnessing that Agamben proposes can be understood as an ethics of survival, in so far as the human survives the inhuman in testimony. He notes that the currents of human and inhuman that cross over within the human being indicate that "life bears with it a caesura that can transform all life into survival and all survival into life" (*RA*: 133). Recalling the discussions of *bios* and *zoē* in *Homo Sacer*, he states in *Remnants of Auschwitz* that "biopower's supreme ambition is to produce, in a human body, the absolute separation of the living being and the speaking being, *zoē* and *bios*, the inhuman and the human – survival" (*ibid.*: 156). In contrast to Foucault, Agamben suggests that the definitional formula of biopower is not "to make live or let die",[13] but rather *to make survive*; that is, to produce bare life as life reduced to survival through the separation of the human from the inhuman. The perceived value of testimony, then, is that it presents an enduring opposition to the separation of human life and survival: "with its every word, testimony refutes precisely this isolation of survival from life" (*RA*: 157). Testimony bears witness to the inhuman in the human and thus prevents their separation and collapse in the production of bare life.

This raises the question of just what Agamben means by the "human" and the "inhuman", and more specifically, how these terms relate to questions of testimony and language. What does Agamben mean, for instance, when he suggests that what is borne witness to is the inhuman? In what way does testimony refute the isolation of survival from life? To get a clearer picture of what Agamben is proposing, some attention must here be given to his account of subjectification, or the process by which the human as living being becomes a subject in language. This account rests on the distinction between the human as a speaking being and as a living being, and their interrelation and disjuncture in speech. In a move that is reminiscent of both Aristotle and Heidegger, Agamben's account of subjectification works with the distinction between the speaking being and living being, where the former of these correlates with the human and the latter correlates with the inhuman.

Agamben understands subjectivity as the "production of consciousness in the event of discourse" (*RA*: 123) and his account of this is developed through theorization of two existential modalities, the first affective and the second linguistic. With regard to the first of these, in taking up Levi's identification of the particular shame felt by survivors of the camps, Agamben argues that shame is the constitutive affective tonality of subjectivity. He rejects interpretations of the shame of the survivor in terms of guilt or innocence to argue that the experience of shame derives not from culpability but from the ontological situation of being consigned to something that one cannot assume. The starting point for Agamben's understanding of shame is Emmanuel Lévinas's claim that shame arises from "our being's incapacity to move away and break from itself" (*ibid.*: 104),[14] evident in for instance the impossible desire to separate oneself from a particular presentation of oneself. Shame is not a consequence of an imperfection or lack from which we separate ourselves, but arises from the sheer impossibility of separating ourselves from ourselves. For example, the shame felt in nudity is not shame at a lack that one perceives in oneself, but a consequence of not being able to present oneself otherwise, of being exposed in a vision from which one seeks to hide.

Extending on this, Agamben argues that shame arises from consignment to something that one cannot assume, but that this something is not external to ourselves but "originates in our own intimacy; it is what is most intimate in us" (*RA*: 105), that is, something from which we cannot separate ourselves, but which, simultaneously, we cannot fully take on or adopt as ours. The dilemma this creates for the subject is one of simultaneous subjectification and desubjectification, wherein the subject is called to witness its own ruin. As Agamben puts it,

> It is as if our consciousness collapsed and, seeking to flee in all directions, was simultaneously summoned by an irrefutable order to be present at its own defacement, at the expropriation of what is most its own. In shame, the subject thus has no other content than its own desubjectification; it becomes witness to its own disorder, its own oblivion as a subject. (*Ibid.*: 106)

The experience or affectivity of shame thus indicates a double movement, whereby subjectification is accompanied by desubjectification, understood as the destitution or ruin of the subject. But this double movement is not an occasional turmoil for the subject; instead, it indicates a fundamental characteristic of subjection itself: the double process of subjectification and desubjectification is the unavoidable condition of being in language (*ibid.*: 107).

Turning to the linguistic modality of subjectification, then, Agamben argues that the taking place of the subject in language is itself an occasion for shame, a claim he develops through an analysis of pronouns and particularly the enunciative event of "I". Returning to the outline of subjectivity and language developed in earlier texts through reference to Benveniste's analysis of pronouns, Agamben argues that pronouns operate as grammatical shifters, or "indicators of enunciation" that have no substantive reference outside of themselves, but that allow a speaker to appropriate and put language to use. Hence terms such as "I" and "you" indicate an appropriation of language without referring to a reality outside of discourse. Instead, their sole point of reference is to language itself, and particularly the very taking place of enunciation. "Enunciation . . . refers not to the *text* of what is stated, but to its *taking place*; the individual can put language into act only on condition of identifying himself with the very event of saying, and not with what is said in it (*RA*: 116). Moreover, the pronoun reveals that the enunciative taking place of speech is riven by a double movement of subjectification and desubjectification, which structures the relation of the subject to the language in which it appears. Put simply, while the appropriation of language allows for the constitution of the subject in language, it also requires that the psychosomatic individual erase or de-subjectify itself as an individual in its identification with grammatical shifters or pronouns. That is, in order to become the subject of enunciation, the individual must effectively obviate itself as the agent of speech.

This has the consequence that the assumption of the position of subject of enunciation does not so much allow access to the possibility of speaking as assert the impossibility of it. As Agamben suggests, this is partly because in becoming the subject of enunciation, the subject finds itself anticipated and preceded by a "glossolalic potentiality over which he has neither control nor mastery" (RA: 116). But more importantly, the enunciative event of "I" indicates that "the subject of enunciation is composed in discourse and exists in discourse alone. But, for this very reason, once the subject is in discourse, he can say nothing; he cannot speak" (ibid.: 116–17). Because the individual is always already distinct from the "I" that gives it a place within language, always other to the "I" of enunciation and, further, because the event of enunciation is itself a pure event in language without reference outside language and thus without meaning, the "I–other" of enunciation is held in the impossibility of speech, of saying anything.

In other words, it is only in the assumption of the grammatical position of "I" as the subject of enunciation that the individual enters into the possibility of speaking. But because that "I" is always already distinct from the individual, it is not the individual who speaks – the individual remains silent. But at the same time, the "I" cannot be the subject of enunciation on its own, since as a grammatical shifter it has no substantive content outside its indication of the event or taking place of enunciation. Consequently, what is at stake in the constitutive desubjectification in subjectification is nothing less than the traditional philosophical definition of the human as a speaking being, or the living being that has language: as "zōon logon echōn". In particular, the nature of the having of language by a living being or the living being's appropriation of language is brought into question and shown to be conditioned by a full expropriation. Agamben states, "the living individual appropriates language in a full expropriation alone, becoming a speaking being only on condition of falling into silence" (RA: 129). Hence the "I" marks the simultaneous appropriation and expropriation of the living being of language and their irreducible disjuncture.

Thus subjectivity is founded on "what is most precarious and fragile in the world: the event of speech" (ibid.: 122). As a consequence of the impossibility of the psychosomatic individual ever fully appropriating language as the site of subjectification, "the fragile text of consciousness incessantly crumbles and erases itself, bringing to light the disjunction on which it is erected: the constitutive desubjectification in every subjectification" (ibid.: 123). Conversely, every desubjectification is attended by the process or event of subjectification, the assumption of the enunciative event of the "I" and the correlative constitution of consciousness in discourse. The double structure in operation here parallels the double movement of subjectification and desubjectification in shame, in that it brings the necessary consignment of the individual to language as a speaking being and the simultaneous impossibility of assuming or taking up the event of speech to light. In this way, shame appears as the principal emotive tonality, or "hidden structure", of subjectivity understood as the constitution of consciousness in the event of discourse, since "insofar as it consists solely in the event of enunciation, consciousness constitutively has the form of being consigned to something that cannot be assumed" (*ibid*.: 128).

This deepens the sense in which shame can be understood as the principal emotive tonality of the subject. But more importantly at this point, it also indicates a fundamental relation between shame and testimony. Since the disjunctive relation of the inhuman and human constitutively has the form of shame, it appears that there is an "intimate" relation between shame and testimony. This means that shame and testimony are inseparable, though they are not co-equal or strictly identifiable. As Agamben puts it, the relation of the living and speaking being has the "form of shame", and this "allows for" testimony, as that which cannot be assigned to a subject but which is nevertheless the subject's only "dwelling place" (*RA*: 130). As the principal tonality or sentiment of ethics, then, shame allows for testimony, but it is also more than this. Shame is effectively the mode by which the subject comes to ethical responsibility, as it were, since the flush of shame is precisely what calls for testimony. As Agamben's discussion of Robert Antelme's story of the young student from Bologna flushing (presumably from shame) in the face of his own death suggests, "that flush is like a mute apostrophe flying through time to reach us, to bear witness to him" (*ibid*.: 104).

Given this account of subjectification and shame, the central questions that Agamben must confront in relation to testimony are simple: who or what speaks? Who bears witness and to whom, or to what? If both the phenomenal individual and the subject of enunciation are rendered silent, then what function does testimony have, and who can fulfil it? Unfortunately, Agamben's response to these questions is enigmatic at best. Ultimately, he posits that it is exactly the disjuncture between the human as living being and speaking being that provides the condition of possibility of testimony. That is, testimony arises in the intimate non-coincidence of the human and inhuman or the speaking being and the living being, the subject and non-subject. As Agamben states, "if there is no articulation between the living being and language, if the 'I' stands suspended in this disjunction, then there can be testimony" (*RA*: 130). As such, testimony marks the fracture of the human being in its own capacity for being human or not-being human, since the "place of the human being is divided . . . the human being exists in the fracture between the living being and the speaking being, the inhuman and the human" (*ibid.*: 134). Moreover, to the extent that this conception of ethics is an ethics of survival, such that the human is the one who survives the inhuman – or rather, survives their own becoming inhuman – then the human is chiasmatically related to the inhuman. That is, in its becoming inhuman, the inhuman again passes into the human. Or, as Agamben writes, "the human being is the inhuman; the one whose humanity has been completely destroyed is the one who is truly human" (*ibid.*: 133). The witness, then, is the remnant or the remainder of the isolation of the inhuman amidst the human and the incapacity to wholly destroy it, such that the inhuman passes over into the epitome of the human.

Two further points should be made about this conception of testimony and the *Muselmann* as the threshold between the human and the inhuman. First, I mentioned earlier that Agamben understands the camps to be a biopolitical experiment on the "operators of Being". By this he means that modal categories such as possibility, impossibility, contingency and necessity are "ontological operators, that is, the devastating weapons used in the biopolitical struggle for Being" and, moreover, "the field of this battle is subjectivity" (*RA*: 146–7). Agamben argues that possibility ("to be able to be") and contingency ("to be able not to be") should be understood as "operators of subjectification" that indicate "the point at which something possible passes into existence". Opposing these are the "operators of desubjectification", impossibility and necessity, both of which entail negation in that the former indicates the negation of being able to be and the latter the negation of being able not to be. As tools in the biopolitical battle for Being, these operators isolate and divide the possible and the impossible in subjectivity; they "divide and separate" the "living being and the speaking being, the Muselmann and the witness".

From this perspective, the devastating novelty of Auschwitz is that it represents the historical point at which "the impossible is forced into the real" and contingency is radically negated. The processes of subjectification and desubjectification collapse such that the *Muselmann* stands as the "catastrophe of the subject", a manifestation of the "subject's effacement as the place of contingency and its maintenance as existence of the impossible" (*RA*: 148). Auschwitz is a biopolitical experiment in making the impossible possible through the negation of the possibility of not-being. From this point of view of the modalities of being and not-being, the camps thus require a fundamental reorientation of Western philosophy and, particularly, the rethinking of the relation between actuality and potentiality that Agamben had earlier posited as the core of the project of overcoming metaphysics. This is one way in which Agamben's account of the internal logic of the camps draws on his earlier work in texts such *Language and Death* and essays in *Potentialities*.

The second point to make also highlights the continuity of Agamben's concerns around language, metaphysics and potentiality through to his analysis of biopolitics. In *Language and Death*, Agamben argues against the tendency in metaphysical thought to presuppose a negative foundation for language, a tendency he diagnoses in Hegel's approach to voice and the question of the ineffable or unspeakable. In response to this, Agamben argues that what is instead required is a thought purified of negativity and thus able to think the *experimentum linguae* of infancy. Similarly, in *Remnants of Auschwitz* Agamben rejects the tendency in Holocaust literature and theories of witnessing to rely on the trope of the ineffable. But this clearly does not mean that he simply argues that one should speak about the Holocaust as a historical event – Levi's paradox refutes that possibility from the start. Instead, Agamben suggests that "because testimony is the relation between a possibility of speech and its taking place, it can exist only through a relation to an impossibility of speech – that is, only as *contingency*, as a capacity not to be" (RA: 145). The impossibility of speech that Agamben references here is not a matter of the ineffable, that which cannot be spoken about or uttered in speech, whether understood as internal or external to language itself. Rather, he invokes the notion of *infancy*, suggesting that *the human being is a speaking being only because it is capable of not having language, that is, "because it is capable of its own in-fancy"* (ibid.: 146, emphasis added).

We saw in Chapter 1 that for Agamben infancy means a muteness or incapacity to speak that is not temporally prior to speech as a developmental stage, but that is ontologically prior and both makes speech possible and is expropriated or set aside in any appropriation of language in speech. We can note here that (according to the *Oxford English Dictionary*), etymologically, the terms "infancy" and "ineffable" are extremely close in that both derive from the Latin *"fari"*, meaning to speak and both take the negating prefix "in-". However, what is distinctive about infancy for Agamben is its association with the modal category of contingency and thus with the *capacity* to speak or not to speak as a distinctive capacity of the human being and, more specifically, as the very possibility of subjectivity. This contingent capacity for speech, and thus incapacity for speech, is both the condition of possibility and object of testimony. Ultimately, then, it is the incapacity to speak, the desubjectification in any subjectification, that is borne witness to in testimony. As Agamben writes, "the authority of the witness consists in his capacity to speak solely in the name of an incapacity to speak – that is, in his or her being a subject" (RA: 158), or "the speech of the witness bears witness to a time in which human beings did not yet speak; and so the testimony of human beings attests to a time in which they were not yet human" (*ibid.*: 162).

Agamben's subsequent formulation that "the witness, the ethical subject, is the subject who bears witness to desubjectification" (*ibid.*: 151) makes clear that while he is primarily interested in the formulation of an ethics of witnessing in relation to the specific conditions of Auschwitz, the scope of his argument actually extends beyond these conditions to generate an account of ethical subjectivity *per se*. This is so because, as an exceptional space, the camps are the "new biopolitical *nomos* of the planet" or the "hidden matrix of the politics in which we are still living" (*HS*: 176, 175; *ME*: 45, 44). That is, to the extent that the camp operates as a paradigm, its singularity yields theoretical insight into ethical subjectivity more generally. Consequently, if the task of witnessing is to bear witness to the impossibility of speaking, or the desubjectification in every subjectification, then it follows that every subject is at least potentially a witness. To the extent that desubjectification is a constitutive condition of subjectification and the subject's taking place in language, the impossibility of fully entering into the enunciative place of the subject always calls to be witnessed. This means that it is only as a subject that the witness can claim any authority to speak of the incapacity to speak, but it also suggests that bearing witness to the impossibility of speaking is one of the definitional capacities of the subject.

However, if the foregoing interpretation of Agamben's account of testimony and shame holds as a general theory of ethical subjectivity, then we are entitled to examine this theory in relation to other competing theories of ethics and responsibility. What value does this account have over and against its competitors that would recommend it as a way of understanding our ethical obligations and responsibilities as human subjects? To address this question, in the remainder of this chapter I consider Agamben's account alongside more established approaches to ethics that he either rejects outright or that are negated by at least some of the claims that he makes in both his theory of ethics and, more generally, his diagnosis of biopolitical nihilism. In doing so, I want to begin to develop two angles of critique of Agamben's formulation of ethics, which will then lead into a discussion of his contribution to an alternative theory of emancipation and political transformation in Chapter 5.

Ethics without law: rights and justice

Through reflection on the camp as a biopolitical experiment on the operators of being, Agamben develops an ethics of testimony based on an unassumable yet unavoidable "non-responsibility". His account of ethical responsibility is premised on a strong rejection of juridical conceptions of responsibility and obligation; as such, he attempts to delimit an unassumable "non-responsibility" that is "beyond culpability and guilt", and that moves away from the presupposition of dignity as the core ethical concept. This rejection of a juridical basis for ethical responsibility is consequent on his earlier critique of law as being in force without significance in *Homo Sacer*. Agamben's strong critique of law and normative discourse in its entirety in this text raises significant questions about the relation of his theorization of ethics and politics to more standard political and ethical or moral discourses, which in broad terms usually involve some conception of rights as a more or less indispensable aspect of the delimitation and protection of political liberties and which, moreover, provide a measure for the attainment of justice in the modern world. Here, I want to focus briefly on the critique of law and juridico-normative thought to, first, provide a clear outline of what Agamben proposes in the place of such thought – that is, the notion of an unassumable non-responsibility – and secondly, to consider some of the ethical and political implications of his outright rejection of discourses of rights, including those of political liberty rights, and jurisprudential conceptions of justice.

The starting point for Agamben's conception of ethics in *Remnants of Auschwitz* is the rejection of what he sees as the common confusion between ethical and juridical concepts, since the latter are inherently and solely directed towards judgement, whereas the former must eschew exactly that tendency. Ethics should instead be directed towards what Agamben, following Spinoza, identifies as the "doctrine of happy life". This shift in the understanding of the internal logic of ethics is significant, since it entails rejecting the concepts that attend juridical judgement, including both guilt and responsibility. As Agamben writes, "ethics is the sphere that recognizes neither guilt nor responsibility . . . To assume guilt and responsibility . . . is to leave the territory of ethics and enter that of law" (*RA*: 24). Of responsibility in particular, Agamben argues that the etymology of the term alerts us to its juridical origin in so far as the Latin term *spondeo* from which the modern concept of responsibility derives indicates "to become the guarantor of something for someone (or for oneself) with respect to someone" (cited in *RA*: 21). Consequently, assuming responsibility for something or someone is at origin a juridical rather than an ethical gesture. "Responsibility is closely intertwined with the concept of *culpa* that, in a broad sense, indicates the imputability of damage . . . Responsibility and guilt thus express simply two aspects of legal imputability" (*ibid.*).

Agamben concludes from this etymological discussion that this indicates the "insufficiency and opacity" of every ethical doctrine that is conceptually

97

contaminated by the law (*ibid.*). But the missing set of premises here is just what is wrong with the law, such that contamination by it renders an ethical discourse obsolete or at least problematic. Here, Agamben is presupposing the critique of law that he develops in *Homo Sacer* and elsewhere. In this, he argues that law in the modern age has entered into a legitimation crisis, summed up in the formula of being in force without significance. Thus in *Homo Sacer*, he writes

> All societies and all cultures today (it does not matter whether they are democratic or totalitarian, conservative or progressive) have entered into a legitimation crisis in which law (we mean by this term the entire text of tradition in its regulative form, whether the Jewish Torah or the Islamic Sharia, Christian dogma or the profane *nomos*) is in force as the pure "Nothing of Revelation".
>
> (HS: 51)

The justification for founding a non-juridical ethics lies in the claim that all law – understood as encompassing all normative or regulative discourse – is struck by the nihilistic crisis of being in force without significance. The sweeping breadth of Agamben's critique evident in this statement has, unsurprisingly, drawn its detractors. Not only does he equate *all* social and cultural forms, but additionally suggests that *all* regulative discourse is struck by the same nihilistic crisis. It is difficult to see how such a claim could be justified (at least beyond its becoming a formalistic argument that then runs the risk of falling into exactly the same trap as it diagnoses).

But if we grant this argument for the moment, we can at least see why Agamben concludes that ethical discourse should be freed from juridical contamination. That is, if all normative or regulative discourse is struck by a legitimation crisis, then to the extent that ethics relies on or is derived from that discourse, it suffers from the same problem. This means that there is an onus on Agamben to provide an alternative set of ethical concepts that supplant the reliance on guilt and responsibility. In this regard, he turns to the idea of an "unassumable non-responsibility". However, if responsibility is "irremediably contaminated by law", the simple reversal of assuming responsibility into its opposite is unimaginative on Agamben's part. This is especially so given that he provides no indication why this negation itself does not already incorporate the juridicism he wishes to avoid. In other words, there is a question about whether the simple turn from responsibility to non-responsibility is sufficient to eradicate all traces of juridicism from the thinking of ethics.

Further, while he suggests the necessity of a "confrontation with a responsibility that is infinitely greater than any we could ever assume" (*RA*:

21), such that all one can do is be faithful to it by asserting its unassumability, there is little further clarification of what such a "non-responsibility" might entail at either a conceptual or practical level. Certainly, the idea of a responsibility that is greater than that which can be assumed by the subject has precedent in the work of Emmanuel Lévinas. He argues throughout his works such as *Otherwise than Being* that responsibility precedes and exceeds the ethical subject and thereby holds the subject hostage to the Other. But Agamben rejects Lévinas's theorization of responsibility on the basis that it "transformed the gesture of the *sponsor* [that is, an originally juridical concept] into the ethical gesture par excellence" (*RA*: 22). That is, rather than escaping the juridical form, Lévinas's ethics presupposes it. Consequently, if it is to be genuinely non-juridical, Agamben cannot derive his understanding of an unassumable non-responsibility from Lévinas. I shall return to a closer examination of the idea of an unassumable non-responsibility and Agamben's rejection of Lévinas's ethics in the following section on subjectivity and responsibility.

But before this, it is worth considering the further implications of Agamben's rejection of juridical concepts within ethics, since this critique also entails abandoning more standard moral and political theories that incorporate or rely on conceptions of rights. Not satisfied with simply cleansing ethics of reference to rights, Agamben also rejects recourse to political rights as a limitation on the violence of biopolitical sovereignty, claiming that because Western politics is a biopolitics from the very beginning, "every attempt to found political liberties in the rights of the citizen is . . . in vain" (*HS*: 181). This argument draws on Hannah Arendt's brief discussion of the doctrine of human rights in her study of totalitarianism and the massive increase in numbers of stateless peoples in World War I and its aftermath. Arendt points out that there is an important connection between the rights of the citizen and human rights, whereby while the latter are supposed to be founded in the very condition of being human, they are in fact only operational within the context of nation-state-guaranteed citizenship rights. Thus she argues that at the very moment at which human rights should have come into effect, stateless peoples and refugees found themselves in a situation of being without rights altogether. The plight of the stateless is not "the loss of specific rights, then, but the loss of a community willing and able to guarantee any rights whatsoever".[15]

Two points about Arendt's claim are especially significant for the way in which Agamben extrapolates from this to his own rejection of human rights in particular, as well as rights discourse more generally. The first of these is the way Arendt questions the status of the human in relation to the citizen. She claims that to the extent that stateless peoples are expelled from political community by virtue of their lack of legal status, their belonging to the human species is akin to the way in which other animals belong to species, that is, merely in terms of biological facticity. In the terms of her political theory developed further in *The Human Condition*, the stateless or refugees are excluded from the realms of action and human artifice – hence from the political as such – and are instead reduced to a condition of "mere existence" or "abstract nakeness". In Agamben's terms, this is roughly equivalent to the status of *zoē*, or mere biological life, although his account of the relation of *bios* (political life) emphasizes the ambiguity between these conditions more than Arendt's does. He also expands this point to emphasize the relation between nation-states and birth, claiming that "nation-state means a state that makes nativity or birth (that is, naked human life) the foundation of its sovereignty" (*ME*: 21). This not only highlights the indistinction between *bios* and *zoē*, but, in doing so, also illuminates for him the intrinsic relation between the natural and the political in nation-state formations, and the conceptions such as rights that they generate and rely on. For Agamben, not only recourse to human rights but any reliance on citizenship rights will necessarily reinscribe this biopolitical relation between sovereignty and natural life.

The second significant point is closely related to this. As Agamben points out, Arendt's chapter on statelessness and human rights is entitled "The Decline of the Nation-State and the End of the Rights of Man". The significance of this is that in so far as rights and the nation-state are inextricably linked, the decline of one also entails the demise of the other. More importantly, though, the explosion of numbers of refugees – initially from World War I but also at an apparently ever-increasing rate – actually contributes to the end of the state by making its foundation in natural life apparent and opening possibilities for a new politics distinct from national sovereignty. That is, while the figure of the refugee should have consolidated human rights, it has instead marked a radical crisis of the concept "by breaking the identity between the human and the citizen and that between nativity and nationality" and bringing sovereignty into crisis (*ME*: 21, 23). The refugee, for Agamben, is a "limit-concept" that brings crisis to nation-state formations and thereby opens the way to a new politics. Citing Arendt's formulation that refugees constitute the "vanguard of the people", Agamben suggests that this is not because they presage the formation of a new state, but because they break the link between state, natality and territoriality, and thus inaugurate the possibility of a new "aterritorial" or "extraterritorial" space of topological indeterminacy. Such a space would entail perforating the interior and exterior (the regulation of which is key to the nation-state, as the recent "refugee crisis" in Western liberal democracies such as Australia and the UK made evident), thereby liberating politics from the nation-state formation and allowing every citizen to recognize the refugee that he or she is (*ibid.*: 23–5).

I shall say more about this conception of a politics beyond the end of the nation-state and biopolitical sovereignty in Chapter 5. But first, two further points can be made about this rejection of rights and critique of law that underpins it. First, this highlights the conceptual and methodological divergence between Foucault and Agamben that I mentioned earlier. While Foucault was also interested in the liberation of politics and political theory from the sovereign state form, his approach to the question of rights is significantly different from Agamben's. For example, in a short document "Confronting Governments: Human Rights", written on the occasion of the formation of an International Committee against Piracy in response to attacks on Vietnamese refugees in the Gulf of Thailand, Foucault does not hesitate to evoke a conception of rights.[16] Albeit written with a particular political purpose in mind, this occasional document calls upon an international citizenry with rights and duties, obliged to speak out against abuses of power in solidarity as members of the community of the governed. In other more theoretically developed remarks, Foucault takes other positions on the question of rights, but in doing so, does not reject rights *tout court*. Instead, he suggests that what is required is a *new form of right* that is no longer tied to sovereignty. In both these approaches, Foucault recognizes the potential tactical value of rights in political struggles.[17]

Second, if Agamben's critique of law, understood to encompass "all regulative discourse", is granted, we can then ask what alternative conception of justice he can offer, since he cannot rely on a jurisprudential conception of it in either a retributive or distributive sense. Interestingly, Agamben says relatively little about the notion of justice, apart from his insistence that justice is irreducible to law: while law might be the path to justice, it is not justice itself. Without going into detail, Agamben's conception of justice is ultimately indebted to both an opposition between justice and the natural world, and the distinction between justice and profane law found in Judaism. In a manner that is crucial to Agamben's own conception of biopolitics and legal violence, Benjamin addresses the triad of law, justice and the natural order in the essay "Critique of Violence". In this, he posits the necessity of a divine violence that destroys mythic, legal violence and expiates the guilt of "mere life". Resisting the reduction of "man" to mere life that the modern conception of the sanctity of life threatens, Benjamin begins to isolate the "not-yet-attained" condition of the just man, who must necessarily exist outside the realm of fate that underlies all manifestations of law and the violence that Benjamin sees as inherent to it. It is exactly this "not-yet-attained" condition of the just that Agamben is attempting to elaborate in his own conception of a life beyond law, beyond the violence of biopolitical sovereignty and beyond the condition of the camps.

The remnant and the other: the non-relationality of Agamben's ethics

Before moving to this notion of a life beyond law, it is worth saying more about the particular conception of ethical subjectivity that Agamben is suggesting. This will help to provide a clearer sense of what he means by an unassumable non-responsibility. As we have seen, Agamben's theorization of the subject's constitution in language as a specifically ethical problem in the form of testimony generates an account of an unassumable yet unavoidable "non-responsibility". On the face of it, this idea would seem to bear some resemblance to Emmanuel Lévinas's account of a responsibility that precedes and exceeds the subject, and which holds the subject hostage to the Other. As we saw in the previous section, though, Agamben's rejection of the juridical form of ethics is thoroughgoing, and includes rejecting Lévinas's formulation. In fact, Agamben accuses Lévinas of making a juridical gesture *par excellence* in understanding ethics as a responsibility or an *obligation* that the subject can never fulfil. For one, this leads to unending guilt. In contrast, Agamben casts *Remnants of Auschwitz* as an attempt to erect "signposts" for the exploration of a new ethical terrain "beyond culpability and guilt".

The *Muselmann* is figured as the threshold between the human and the inhuman, and, as such, puts into question any ethics based upon that distinction. Testimony arises, then, in the disjuncture and indistinction of the human and inhuman, revealed in the simultaneous processes of subjectification and desubjectification at work in the human being's entering into language in the enunciative event of "I". This in turn reveals that shame is the principal affective tonality of the subject. Interestingly, at one point in *Remnants of Auschwitz*, it seems that it is the affect of shame that carries the imperative to bear witness – where the flush of shame is figured through something "like" an unavoidable apostrophe that calls us to bear witness. But Agamben's figuration of the flush of shame as an apostrophe – a rhetorical gesture in which the text calls directly to the reader and thereby interpolates the reader into the text itself – points us towards an important question to which Agamben does not, and perhaps cannot, provide a convincing response. That is, how can Agamben's theorization of an ethical non-responsibility account for the relational dimensions of responsibility and ethical subjectivity?

In general terms, ethics can be understood as delimiting the way in which we can or should act in our relations towards others. In this, ethics seems to pick out the specifically relational aspect of our being and acting in the world. This relational dimension of ethics carries throughout various theories, although it is given different weight and significantly different formulations within each. But even a theory such as utilitarianism – which on the face of it presupposes a more or less atomistic individual as its starting point – presupposes some kind of relationality in its formulation of enhancing *overall* well-being. In fact, it has been argued that one of the problems with utilitarianism is that it fails to sufficiently disaggregate the individual. Of course, the ontology of ethical subjectivity on which utilitarianism is based does not allow a fundamental role to relationality in the way that some ethical theories – in particular, that of Lévinas – argue must be the case. For Lévinas, relationality is not merely the context of ethical decision-making, but is constitutive of ethical subjectivity from the start. The fundamental role of relationality is established in his conception of proximity, which is also tightly integrated with language.

Lévinas's ethics begin from an irreducible proximity of human subjects with one another, and this relation of proximity and alterity is what constitutes the humanity of the human being. In this, the alterity of the Other presents an imperative of responsibility that precedes and exceeds the subject, such that the Other holds the ethical subject hostage. This relation of command and hostage is particularly figured through the face-to-face encounter, in which one is exposed to the other in vulnerability. Within this construal of responsibility, Lévinas rejects a view of language as a simple means of communication or manifestation of truth in content. Instead, he argues that language originates in the non-verbal command of the face-to-face encounter and, as such, the relation of the subject to language is one of a fundamental passivity. Further, this construal means that language is necessarily and irrevocably tied to alterity.

Agamben's approach to ethical subjectivity is similar to that of Lévinas in so far as he also works from the "radical passivity" of the subject in relation to language.[18] But while referencing Lévinas, Agamben's account of an unassumable non-responsibility also differs in its treatment of alterity and relationality. While these are ineradicable aspects of responsibility and ethical subjectivity for Lévinas, Agamben, in contrast, appears to neglect or even exclude any sense of a fundamental relationality within ethics. This is despite the fact that the notions of witnessing and testimony would seem to require at least some articulation of intersubjective relations. If Agamben can be read in the way that I am suggesting, it seems that he avoids precisely the problem that "bearing witness" would intuitively entail – that is, the relation of the living to the dead, or, more generally, the relation of the subject to others. He seems to avoid the question of relationality within ethics, although such a question is intuitively central to the problematic of bearing witness.[19] Several aspects of Agamben's discussion of testimony and shame indicate that it excludes relationality.

First, given the formulation of shame as the form of the relation of the inhuman and human within the single existent, it is not clear that an ethics of witnessing extends beyond an auto-affection, in which the subject acts solely in relation to its own passivity. Indeed, Agamben casts shame as precisely a matter of auto-affection, wherein the "agent and patient [coincide] in one subject" (*RA*: 111). That auto-affection is central to Agamben's ethics of testimony is also indicated by his suggestion noted earlier that testimony arises in the double processes of subjectification and desubjectification, wherein the subject is called to witness its *own* ruin in shame. Interestingly, this process of auto-affection is said to produce the *self* as its remainder. Although Agamben gives little indication of what he means by the "self" in this context, beyond indicating that it is conceptually distinct from the "subject", this again highlights the centrality of auto-affection. For here, the constitution of self requires no more than the subject's relation to itself in subjectification and desubjectification.

Secondly, following on from this, we can consider Agamben's construal of subjectivity and language more directly, particularly through the use he makes of the idea of pronouns as grammatical shifters. We have seen that "I" indicates the taking place of enunciation itself, and in so doing marks the dual processes of subjectification and desubjectification that the living being must endure in appropriating language and becoming a speaking being. What Agamben fails to take into account, though, is that the taking place of enunciation can itself be seen as always a matter of "being-with" others,[20] in so far as grammatical shifters do not simply indicate the double movement of subjectification and desubjectification, but also the position of the subject in relation to others. That is, the living being's entering into language through the designation of pronouns does not simply indicate the position of the individual *vis-à-vis* language, but also necessarily indicates the position of the individual in relation to other living and speaking beings. Pronouns such as "I" – and "you" – necessarily position the speaking subject in relation with those being addressed or identified. Moreover, these enunciative positions can only be acceded to in the presence of others: it is only in the context of being with others that one can appropriate language as speaking subject. The enunciative event of pronouns requires the presence of others as a necessary accompaniment to the accession to speech in becoming a subject.

Given this construal of the evasion of questions of relationality within Agamben's work, the question then becomes whether he simply neglects it, or whether his conceptual framework excludes or precludes consideration of relationality and alterity. If the former, then his theorization of an ethical non-responsibility that is not reliant on juridical concepts could be supplemented or corrected to take this into account. If the latter, then – if we accept that relationality and alterity are fundamental aspects of ethics – it would seem that there is a fatal flaw in Agamben's conceptual apparatus. In Chapter 5, I shall suggest that the latter of these interpretations is the correct one. I shall discuss Agamben's formulation of a life beyond law, beyond biopolitics and nihilism, and his conception of "whatever singularity", which he poses as the resolution to the distinction between identity and difference. I shall show that these ideas of "form-of-life" or "whatever singularity" are based on the appropriation of *logos* as that which articulates and folds being. Or, to put the point differently, I shall show that what Agamben seeks is a return to the barrier (/) itself that separates and articulates identity and difference.

CHAPTER FIVE

Messianism: time, happiness and completed humanity

Marx says that revolutions are the locomotive of world history. But perhaps it is quite otherwise. Perhaps revolutions are an attempt by the passengers on this train – namely, the human race – to activate the emergency brake.[1]

As we saw in Chapter 3, Agamben's diagnosis and critique of contemporary juridico-political conditions revolves around the notion of bare life. Obscure as this concept seems at times, it provides not only the central axis for his analysis of exceptional politics, but also the starting point for a theorization of a way beyond contemporary nihilism and the violence of biopolitical capture and abandonment. The notion of bare life develops from the distinction that Aristotle makes between *zoē*, or biological life, and *bios*, or a specified way of life within a political community. At its most conceptually specific, bare life is life suspended between the natural and the political, or natural life included in politics through its exclusion and, as such, infinitely abandoned to sovereign violence. In its position of suspension in relation to sovereign violence, bare life cannot provide a basis for a politics and thought beyond biopolitical sovereignty for Agamben. Instead, any attempt to found a politics on bare life will merely repeat the aporias of modern democracy, which fails in its attempts to reconcile *zoē* and *bios*, and in doing so, continues to produce bare life as the life of political subjects. Given this characterization of bare life, Agamben goes on to indicate that what is required to provide a "unitary centre" for a coming politics is a way of thinking the concept of life that no longer operates within the terrain of *bios* and *zoē*.

Instead, what is required is a happy, reconciled life in which *bios* and *zoē* can no longer be distinguished. As we saw in Chapter 3, Agamben refers to this as "happy life" or "form-of-life" that has reached the perfection of its own power and its own communicability (*ME*: 114–15), and that is consequently beyond the grasp of sovereignty and right. Provocative as this suggestion is, one of the immediate difficulties with the notion of a happy life that any attempt to elaborate it must confront is that Agamben himself provides no real explanation of what he means by this idea. Instead, there are occasional glimpses of what the notion may mean, as well as a number of refractory theorizations that throw light on the idea without necessarily explicitly addressing it. We can be sure, though, that it does not refer to any kind of psychological or emotive state, since, for one, he tends to reject recourse to psychological substance in his theory of the subject. Just as infancy does not refer to a stage of human development, but to a more fundamental condition of being without language while nevertheless capable of speaking, so Agamben's description of a form-of-life as happy also relates to issues of potentiality and its preservation. This conception of a happy life raises a number of issues that draw on and extend various other elements of Agamben's thought, including issues of potentiality, history and his understanding of a coming politics, as well as the concept of the human.

In order to develop a sense of what happy life might amount to, it is necessary to gain a broader sense of Agamben's project for a "coming politics". It is only through this that the notion of happy life can be properly assessed. In this chapter, I elaborate the notion of a happy life over which sovereignty no longer has a hold, and show the way in which it relates to other elements of Agamben's thought. I suggest throughout this chapter that the notion of happy life, or form-of-life, is one of several formulations of Agamben's theory of political liberation; others are the idea of an "unsavable" life and the notion of "whatever being" developed in *The Coming Community*. Different as they may appear, all these ideas are underpinned by a concern with politics understood as the suspension of the relation between means and end – that is, a *politics of pure means* in which the instrumentality of contemporary politics and thought is suspended through a new relation to and *new use* of objects, ideas and, most significantly, law itself. This idea of a new use of law is suggested in Agamben's discussions of play and profanation, and it leads to a conception of justice as a new relation to the forgotten or lost past that has never been. Throughout his discussions of a "coming politics" Agamben also insists upon the idea of the historical appropriation of the *ethos* of humanity, and the perceived necessity of a conception of time appropriate to the messianic task of contemporary politics. This chapter elaborates these various threads of Agamben's approach to happiness and the nature of post-historical humanity.

Post-historical humanity: happiness, "form-of-life" and the unsavable

The fact that the ancient Greeks did not have a unified concept of life and instead isolated and identified several variants proves to be highly productive for Agamben's own thinking about the concept of life. His point of reference in relation to the Greek differentiations of life is typically Aristotle, in either the *Politics* or *De Anima*. In the first of these texts, Aristotle defines and differentiates life in relation to the political community, suggesting that whereas the household is most closely associated with the life of reproduction, in contrast the *polis* is most concerned not with life *per se*, but with the good life – not living, but living well. For Agamben, this distinction between natural life and political forms of life is first and foremost the starting point for the emergence of biopolitical sovereignty that includes life in politics only through its exclusion. Thus the danger of biopolitics is not that it collapses forms-of-life into natural life as is often supposed but, rather, that it relentlessly separates one from the other. This separation of *zoē* and *bios* provides the conceptual condition for the production of bare life as "natural life exposed to death". Thus, as it is formulated in *Homo Sacer*, Aristotle's division provides the conceptual *arthron* that drives the originary biopolitical structure of Western politics.

That this distinction lies behind the production of bare life is also the theoretical starting point for Agamben's positive theory of political liberation, since, he argues, a coming politics must consequently be founded on a conception of life in which such a distinction is no longer possible. Perhaps the clearest formulation of this idea appears in a short essay in *Means without End*, where Agamben posits the necessity of a "life that can never be separated from its form, a life in which it is never possible to isolate something such as naked life" (*ME*: 3–4). The "form-of-life" that Agamben identifies as the necessary point of departure for a politics distinct from any form of sovereignty is a life of pure potentiality, in which "what is at stake in its way of living is living itself ", by which he means that "the single ways, acts and processes of living are never simply *facts* but always and above all *possibilities* of life, always and above all power" (*ibid.*: 4). This construal of "form-of-life" in which life appears as pure possibility recalls Agamben's approach to potentiality that I discussed in Chapter 1, in which he emphasizes the suspension of the transition from potential to act, and the maintenance of impotentiality within potentiality. It also recalls his figuration of a child suspended in its totipotency, or its lack of specification in relation to a particular environment and thereby open to the world as such. Such an infant is for Agamben characterized by its being its own potentiality or living its own possibility, such that "one no longer distinguishes between possibility and reality, but turns the possible into life itself" (FPI).

Thus the infant existing in its own possibility without being given over to a particular environment provides a key example of "form-of-life" for Agamben. No doubt, the construal of infantile being as totipotent is questionable for its abstraction from the social and normative conditions of existence that constrain and produce in a more or less rigid fashion the possibilities for living that any child has available to it.[2] But the more important point to make here concerns the formulation that Agamben uses to understand the potentiality of the infant – that it is truly thrown outside itself into the world, rather than into a specific environment. This formulation is important, as it is exactly the question of the relation of the human to the world and to a specific environment that is at issue in Agamben's short book, *The Open*. In what is structurally an incomplete essay on Martin Heidegger with a coda on Walter Benjamin, Agamben provides perhaps his most elaborate reflection on the nature of happy life, which is ultimately formulated as life that is saved by virtue of being unsavable.

The Open takes up Aristotle's differentiation of life in *De Anima* to suggest that this indicates that "life" has no positive content as such, but that the division of life "passes first of all as a mobile border within living man" and, as such, provides the necessary condition for the decision on what is human. It is by virtue of the division of life that a hierarchy of vegetal, animal and human life, and the economy of relations between them, can be established. Because of this, the question of life itself turns into a question of humanism, or, to put it more carefully, any attempt to think the concept of life outside the frame given to Western philosophy by Aristotle and the divisions it institutes will necessarily entail questioning the presuppositions of humanism, of what it is to be human and what relation of distance and proximity the being so identified bears to those excluded from that designation. In this, then, Agamben's reflections in *The Open* turn toward Heidegger's extended concern with humanism. Agamben's target is most explicitly the particular mode of being of the human as opposed to other animals, as discussed in *The Fundamental Concepts of Metaphysics*, but his engagement can also be read as a response to Heidegger's essay "Letter on Humanism".

In this essay, in response to questions about his perceived anti-humanism, Heidegger reiterates the importance of humanism while also rejecting it in so far as the humanistic tradition has failed to set the measure of the essence of man sufficiently high. That is, in so far as it remains caught within the metaphysical tradition that only thinks beings, humanism fails to recognize the unique position of man in relation to the "clearing of Being" and attunement to world. This failure of humanism derives from the attempt to understand the essence of man from the direction of animality – that is, as a rational animal. For Heidegger, this approach is always conditioned by metaphysics, since "metaphysics thinks of man on the basis of *animalitas* and does not think in the direction of his *humanitas*".[3] But, as such, it fails to understand that "what man is . . . lies in his ek-sistence", that he is "the there, that is, the clearing of Being" (229). Consequently, while other living creatures are close to *Dasein*, they are nevertheless "separated from our ek-sistent essence by an abyss" (230). That is, "because plants and animals are lodged in their respective environments but are never freely in the clearing of Being which alone is 'world', they lack language", where "language is not the utterance of an organism; nor is it the expression of a living thing"; "[it] is the clearing-concealing advent of Being itself" (230).

Heidegger's double movement of critique and recuperation of humanism can be seen as the target of Agamben's reflections in *The Open*, and, in this light, the ambivalence of his relation to the German philosopher becomes apparent. For while similarly emphasizing the urgency of first philosophy in relation to political *praxis*, Agamben implicitly rejects Heidegger's attempt to set humanism on a new non-metaphysical footing, suggesting that humanism is a "fundamental metaphysico-political operation in which alone something like 'man' can be decided upon and produced" (O: 21). For Agamben, the "anthropological machine of humanism" not only fails to measure the human appropriately, but is itself the very thing that produces the human and, in doing so, ironically "verifies the absence of a nature proper to *Homo*" (*ibid*.: 29). But if Agamben wishes to move beyond the Heideggarian conception of man as *Dasein*, distinct from other living creatures by virtue of his essence in *ek-sistence*, then two aspects of his theorization require further exploration: first, how does he set Heidegger aside, and, secondly, what does he propose instead?

For the first of these, Agamben's approach is to show that the distinction between animals and men that Heidegger indicates in "Letter on Humanism" and in more detail in *The Fundamental Concepts of Metaphysics* does not hold since each side of the distinction is contaminated by the other. Moreover, he contends that Heidegger does not move beyond the metaphysical understanding of humanism, and, as such, proves limited in the necessity of stopping the anthropological machine that continually produces the human as that being without its own nature. Heidegger's thesis in *Fundamental Concepts* is that while man or *Dasein* is world-forming, animals are "poor in world" in that they are deprived of access to beings as beings among others. This does not mean that animals are wholly without world, as is the case with a stone, since deprivation relies on and presupposes the possibility of access to being; that is, deprivation of something entails *being able to have* but not having something. Poverty in world thus

111

means that the animal is capable of access to the being of beings, but does not actually have that access. The reason for this deprivation lies in the animal's mode of relating to other things, which Heidegger argues is characterized by *captivation* or a *being taken* by those things. Through a complex discussion of Heidegger's characterization of the captivation and poverty of the animal, Agamben concludes that in this view, the ontological status of the animal in its environment can be summarized as being open but not disconcealed, that they are open in an "inaccessibility and an opacity, that is . . . in a nonrelation" (O: 55).

From this "openness without disconcealment" that defines the animal's poverty in world, Agamben turns to the discussion of profound boredom as a fundamental *Stimmung* of the being of *Dasein* to show man's own proximity to this non-relation. In boredom, the proximity of the animal and human is revealed by *Dasein*'s being riveted to beings that refuse themselves. That is, "In becoming bored, Dasein is delivered over to something that refuses itself, exactly as the animal, in its captivation, is exposed in something unrevealed" (O: 65). Moreover, the second "structural moment" of boredom – "being-held-in-suspense" – both reinforces this proximity of *Dasein* and the animal and indicates the step that boredom allows beyond it. This is because "being-held-in-suspense" is the "experience of the disconcealing of the originary possibilization (that is, pure potentiality) in the suspension and withholding of all concrete and specific possibilities" (*ibid.*: 67). What distinguishes *Dasein* from the animal is this possibility of suspending the non-relation of captivation and thereby revealing an originary possibilization or pure potentiality distinct from any particular or factical possibility.

Concluding his discussion of profound boredom and captivation, Agamben argues that "the jewel set at the centre of the human world . . . is nothing other than animal captivation" (*ibid.*: 68). But what distinguishes the human from the animal is its capacity to suspend this captivation, thus allowing the "appearing of undisconcealment as such". Consequently the human and animal are not radically distinct, for "the irresolvable struggle between unconcealedness and concealedness, between disconcealment and concealment, which defines the human world, is the internal struggle between the human and animal" (*ibid.*: 69). But Agamben is not satisfied with simply having shown that man and animal are not "separated by an abyss", as Heidegger argues they are. This is not to say that he urges a return to a biologistic understanding of the human as simply another animal, albeit one with unique capacities such as reason and language. On this point, Agamben accepts Heidegger's critique; but he wishes to push what he sees as the necessarily metaphysico-political doctrines of humanism further to the side than Heidegger does.

In regard to the second question as to what he poses in the stead of Heidegger's approach to humanism, then, his response is complex. At the end of the discussion of Heidegger, Agamben proposes that approaching the question of man and animal from this direction provides two options: first, rather than maintaining his animality as undisclosable, man takes on and governs it through technology; or, secondly, man can appropriate his animality as pure abandonment – that is, as the "shepherd of being" he appropriates his own concealedness and thinks (and *experiences*) it as such. In relation to the first of these options, Agamben maintains a sceptical position, contending that it is unclear whether a humanity that undertakes total management of its own animality is still human. This is because from a Heideggerian perspective, such a humanity "no longer has the form of keeping itself open to the undisconcealed of the animal, but seeks rather to open and secure the not-open in every domain, and thus closes itself to its own openness, forgets its *humanitas*, and makes being its specific disinhibitor" (O: 77). As such, this option undermines the avowed aim of Heidegger's thought to move beyond the metaphysical conception of humanism, which thinks humanity from the direction of animality and not from the direction of his *humanitas*.

However, the second option frames the remaining chapters of *The Open*, in which Agamben turns to Benjamin as a way of thinking pure abandonment, not as a reconciliation of man and animal, but in order to bring about a "new and more blessed life, one that is neither animal nor human", which is "beyond both nature and knowledge, beyond concealment and disconcealment" (O: 87). This life is not redeemed or reconciled in the sense of simply reintegrating natural and non-natural life through, for instance, reducing one to the other. Instead, it is "outside of being", that is, external to the Heideggerian opposition of animal and man on the basis of the openness to being, and instead characterized by beatitude or happiness.

Agamben begins *The Open* with a short reflection on a miniature from a Hebrew Bible from the thirteenth century, which represents the "messianic banquet of the righteous on the last day" (O: 1). What interests Agamben is that the miniature represents the righteous or "concluded humanity" with animal heads, which could suggest that "on the last day, the relations between animals and men will take on a new form, and that man himself will be reconciled with his animal nature" (*ibid.*: 3). While this might be taken as an indication of the direction that Agamben's own thesis in *The Open* will take, this is in fact not the case. Instead, he argues that this representation of the "remnant . . . of Israel, that is, of the righteous who are still alive at the moment of the Messiah's coming" (*ibid.*: 2), does not indicate or prefigure a new "declension of the man–animal relation" (*ibid.*: 92). Instead, it indicates the possibility of stopping the "anthropological machine" that operates through the differentiation between man and animal, and the emergence of a new blessed life in the aftermath of its being rendered inoperative. In short, for Agamben, the "in-human" life that the inoperativity of the anthropological machine allows for is saved precisely by its being unsavable.

Interestingly, Benjamin provides Agamben with a "hieroglyph" of this new "in-humanity" in his figuration of sexual fulfilment in "One-Way Street". In an aphorism entitled "Doctor's Night Bell", Benjamin writes that sexual fulfilment "delivers the man from his secret", which is "comparable to the fetters that bind him to life". The role of a woman in this is to cut these fetters, whereupon "man is free to die because his life has lost its secret. Thereby he is reborn, and as his beloved frees him from the mother's spell, the woman literally detaches him from Mother Earth – a midwife who cuts that umbilical cord which is woven of nature's mystery".[4] Of this, Agamben suggests that Benjamin's vision allows for the recognition of a non-nature through the man's separation or severance from nature. But this separation is not simply a disavowal or rejection of nature, of natural life; rather it is a *"transvaluation"*, which sets natural life up as the "archetype of *beautitudo*" or happiness. The name that Benjamin gives to this nature after transvaluation, in which nature is returned to itself through man's separation from it, is the "saved night". But the salvation at stake here is not one of reintegration of the natural and non-natural through the reappropriation of that which is lost or forgotten. Rather, the "saved night" comes about by virtue of its relation to the unsavable, the lost or forgotten as such – that is, to the wholly profane natural life from which man is separated in sexual fulfilment. Relating this back to the anthropological machine of humanism, Agamben concludes that "In their fulfilment, the lovers who have lost their mystery contemplate a human nature rendered perfectly inoperative – the inactivity and *desœuvrement* of the human and of the animal as the supreme and unsavable figure of life" (O: 87).

Several points can be made about this conception of sexual fulfilment and notion of the "saved night" as they relate to Agamben's conception of human nature. First, it is worth noting that Agamben is unconcerned by the highly gendered (and heterosexist) aspects of the conception of salvation and happiness that this "hieroglyph of a new inhumanity" induces. In fact, this gender-blindness is consistent throughout Agamben's work. For instance, he is also silent on issues of gender in his reference to Aristotle's distinction between the life of the *oikos* and politics, even though gender is insistently present in the designation of the *oikos* as the domain of reproduction that necessarily precedes and supports the life of politics. As Derrida remarks, the distinction of *bios* and *zoē* is not as straightforward as Agamben takes it to be.[5] Additionally, Agamben's construal of gender and the liberatory function of sexual fulfilment is pre-empted in *Idea of Prose*, particularly in a fragment entitled "Idea of Communism". The primary focus of this fragment is pornography, in which the utopia of a classless society is said to appear in the "gross caricatures" of all markers of class and their transformation in the sexual act, itself the necessary conclusion of any pornographic film. The "eternal political justification" for pornography, Agamben argues, is its capacity to reveal the presence of pleasure in everyday life, even if the pleasure that it brings to light is only temporary and fleeting. Pornography "does not elevate the everyday world to the everlasting heaven of pleasure", and necessarily remains limited to revealing the "inner aimlessness of every universal". He goes on to conclude that "pornography achieves its intention" in "representing the pleasure of the woman, inscribed solely in her face" (*IP*: 74).

There is of course a long philosophical tradition of casting women as the privileged figures of ephemerality, unable to gain access to the universal (but nevertheless instrumental in man's access to it). Related to this, there is also a long tradition of positing women's closer relation to the physiological or biological, which Agamben also does in his attempt to articulate a philosophy of infancy. Here, he suggests that women are not unlike the child, who "adheres so closely to its physiological life that it becomes indiscernible from it" (FPI). For anyone with some knowledge of the past several decades of feminist philosophy, it is hard to read such a statement from a contemporary philosopher without some dismay. While Agamben frequently touches on questions of gender in this manner, he does not at any point offer an analysis of gender as part of his figurations of sexual fulfilment and happiness. The point here is not to simply note the general neglect of gender or the exclusion of women from the Agamben's philosophical lexicon at an explicit textual level. The consistent use of gender-specific pronouns as if their reference were universal is surely indicative of a philosophical blindness or "amnesia", but it does not reach the depths of the problem.[6] We have to ask: what would it be to address questions of gender, and by extension other forms of difference such as sexuality, race and class, within the conceptual framework that motivates Agamben's theory of political liberation? Indeed, can such questions be asked within that framework? I consider this issue in more detail in the following sections of this chapter, where I discuss the notion of a politics of pure means and the related concepts of "whatever being" and profanation.

The second point to note about Agamben's reference to Benjamin and the "saved night" is the explicitly *messianic* orientation that it signals. The opening paragraphs of *The Open* – on the remnant of Israel represented with animal heads on the Last Day – set the stage for the later messianic figuration of that which is saved by virtue of being unsavable. But the messianic dimension of Agamben's conception of happiness is made clearer in his reference to Benjamin's short text "Theological–Political Fragment". In this, Benjamin explicitly addresses the relation of messianic and historic time and writes that "[o]nly the Messiah himself completes all history, in the sense that he alone redeems, completes, creates its relation to the Messianic".[7] Constructing an image of two arrows pointing in opposite directions but which are nevertheless reinforcing, Benjamin goes on to say that "the secular order should be erected on the idea of happiness". This is because while the profane cannot in itself establish a relation with the messianic, it assists the coming of the messianic kingdom precisely by being secular or profane. In other words, while the profane is not a category of the messianic, it is "the decisive category of its most unobtrusive approach", because "the rhythm of Messianic nature is happiness".[8] Happiness allows for the fulfilment of historical time, since the messianic kingdom is "not the goal but the terminus" of history.[9] Agamben's absolutely profane happy life draws on this characterization of the profane and the messianic, wherein the profane happy life provides a passage for messianic redemption. In doing so, it also proposes a new understanding of the messianic fulfilment of history as a basis for an understanding of a completed humanity. It is to the issues of time, history and messianic fulfilment that we now turn.

The time of the now: history, *kairos* and the messiah

While attention to the messianic is a consistent feature of much of Agamben's work, particularly the later, more politically oriented texts, his approach to messianism is most explicitly and most thoroughly articulated in *The Time That Remains*. In this, he proposes an interpretation of Pauline theology that emphasizes its messianic dimension, and argues that Paul's "Letter to the Romans" actually aligns conceptually with the messianic threads that run through the thought of Walter Benjamin. Focusing most specifically on Benjamin's text "On the Concept of History", Agamben avers that Benjamin reappropriates Pauline messianism, which itself should be understood as concerning not the founding of a new religion, but the abolition or fulfilment of Jewish law. A number of aspects of Agamben's *œuvre* are thus brought together, often in ways that reinterpret and reformulate earlier concerns and claims, and that make clear his sustained but evolving engagement with questions of history, origin and time, especially as they relate to political theory.

Although we shall not explore its full density, Benjamin's collection of aphorisms in "On the Concept of History" provides us with the clearest starting point for an understanding of Agamben's own theorization of history. Benjamin's main target in these aphorisms is a "historicism" or "universal history" that emphasizes progression, unity and continuity, in the place of which he proposes a theologically inspired conception of historical materialism. For Benjamin, the historicist doctrines of progression and boundless perfectibility condemn humanity to "progression through empty homogenous time"[10] and, as such, necessarily fail to grasp history in its redemptive power. In contrast, historical materialism is precisely the means by which that power can be grasped, since "the historical materialist determines the presence of a messianic force in history".[11] In one of the most famous images from these aphorisms, Benjamin construes a "winning combination" of historical materialism derived from Marxism and theology, in which the latter is the "small and ugly" hunchbacked dwarf that pulls the strings of the puppet called historical materialism. Thus revolutionary politics are tied to, and moreover motivated by, the invisible master of theology.

The importance of this conception of historical materialism for Benjamin is its capacity to release the irruptive power of the historical moment through properly grasping its relation to the present. As Benjamin writes in the seventh thesis, this does not mean recognizing the past moment "as it really was". Instead, it means "appropriating a memory as it flashes up in a moment of danger".[12] The past appears as a fleeting image, which historical materialism attempts to grasp and wrest free of the weight of conformism epitomized by progressivism. The historical image is not to be aligned with a temporal continuum or narrative of past–present–future, but is appropriated to "blast open the continuum of history". The historical moment allows for an irruption in the "empty homogeneous time" to which historicism condemns humanity, since it is the site of a "time filled full by now-time [*Jeztzeit*]" (395). As such, the present cannot simply be understood as a moment of transition between the past and future. Instead, it is an open possibility or opportunity for the appropriation of a past, and thus the constitution of it as properly historical; as Benjamin writes, this "establishes a conception of the present as now-time shot through with the splinters of messianic time" (397). Benjamin's own references to revolution are the best way to exemplify this: rather than simply being the result of preceding causal processes, revolution appears as the appropriation of a past image and "grasping a favourable opportunity" in order to release the messianic power of the present. It is a "leap in the open air of history" (395).

Benjamin's theses on history, particularly his conception of "now-time" and his understanding of historical materialism, provide an important reference point for much of Agamben's own approach to history and time. This is evident from as early as *Infancy and History*, in which Agamben addresses the perceived necessity of a new conception of time adequate to the revolutionary conception of history outlined by Marxism. Picking up on Karl Marx's characterization of man as fundamentally historical, Agamben comments that while Marx did not elaborate a conception of time adequate to this recognition, he nevertheless could not simply take recourse to a linear conception of it as the continual succession of instants. But in so far as this is the predominant conception of time in the West, then the dilemma of modern man is that "he does not yet have an experience of time adequate to his idea of history, and is therefore painfully split between his being-in-time as an elusive flow of instants and his being-in-history, understood as the original dimension of man" (*IH*: 100). Taking up the task of elaborating an idea of time that does not reiterate the instant as its fundamental unit, Agamben turns to alternative sources such as Gnosticism and Stoicism, but also both Benjamin and Heidegger, to emphasize the disruption of time and man's fulfilment as resurrection or decision in that moment.

The model for this conception of time, he suggests, is the notion of *kairos* "the abrupt and sudden conjunction where decision grasps opportunity and life is fulfilled in the moment" (*IH*: 101). Represented as a young man running on his toes, with a long forelock but bald at the back of his head, the figure of *Kairos* personifies fleeting opportunity, which can be grasped as it approaches but not once it has passed. Opposed to time as *chronos*, *kairos* signifies the propitious and fleeting moment that one must take hold of or forever let pass; it is a "between time" which is nevertheless full of possibility. Interestingly, Agamben suggests that we all have a prosaic experience of *kairos* in pleasure or happiness, since it is "only as a source and site of happiness that history can have a meaning for man", where history is not "man's servitude to continuous linear time, but man's liberation from it: the time of history and the *cairos* in which man, by his initiative, grasps favourable opportunity and chooses his own freedom in the moment" (*ibid.*: 104). Thus, Agamben continues, "[j]ust as the full, discontinuous, finite and complete time of pleasure must be set against the empty, continuous and infinite time of vulgar historicism, so the chronological time of psuedo-history must be opposed by the cairological time of authentic history" (*ibid.*: 104–5). With this rejection of chronological time in favour of the "cairological" as the moment of authentic history in mind, we can now turn to Agamben's more recent discussion of time, in which he draws together Pauline messianism and Benjaminian historical materialism to give an extended account of the "between time", or the time that remains.

In *The Time That Remains*, Agamben specifies messianic time as distinct from both the time of prophecy, which is always future referential and announces the coming of the Messiah, and from the *eschaton*, or the eschatological concern with the Last Day and End of Time. Taking up Paul's term for the messianic event – *ho nyn kairos*, or "the time of the now" – Agamben develops a conception of messianic time as neither irremediably "to come" nor the End of Time, but instead a "time that contracts itself and begins to end . . . time that remains between time and its end" (*TR*: 62). This conception of a time contracting itself is best articulated for Agamben through the notion of "operational time" developed by the linguist Gustave Guillaume. Guillaume proposes "operational time" as a way of isolating the time that it takes for the human mind to construct an image of time, to which the actual image constructed is always referred back. Thus Guillaume generates a new "chronogenetic" representation of time that is no longer linear, but three-dimensional. It allows time to grasped as "a pure state of potentiality", alongside "its very process of formation" and "in the state of having been constructed" (*TR*: 66). This means that in so far as humans construct and represent chronological time, in doing so, they produce another time that is not a supplement to chronology, but is internal to the very process of understanding time as chronological.

Relating this to the problem of messianic time, Agamben suggests that it yields a definition of messianic time, in that it is not end time nor futural time, but, rather, "the time we take to bring [time] to an end, to achieve our representation of time"; "messianic time *is the time that time takes to come to an end*" (*TR*: 67). But as such, messianic time is not external to or opposed to chronological time – it is internal to it, and is that which *contracts* chronological time and begins to bring it to an end. This contraction of time, Agamben suggests, is rather like the muscular contraction of an animal before it leaps. While not the leap itself, messianic time is akin to that contraction that makes the leap possible; it is the time "left to us" before the end and which brings about the end. As *kairos*, the time of the now, this operational time is neither identifiable with nor opposed to chronological time, but is instead internal to it as a seized and contracted *chronos* – as "the pearl embedded in the ring of chance" *kairos* is "a small portion of *chronos*, a time remaining" (*TR*: 69). Thus, according to Agamben, Pauline messianism identifies two heterogeneous times – "one *kairos* and one *chronos*, one an operational time and the other a representational time", the relation of which is identified in the term "*para-ousia*", which literally means next to, and more specifically, being beside being, being beside itself. In this way, messianic time "lies beside itself, since, without ever coinciding with a chronological instant, and without ever adding itself onto it, it seizes hold of the instant and brings it forth to fulfilment" (*ibid.*: 71). Agamben avers that the result of this, as Benjamin writes in "On the Concept of History", is that every moment is "the small gateway in time through which the Messiah might enter".[13]

A brief contrast of Agamben's account of the messianic with two other important ways of approaching questions of time and history in recent European philosophy can help bring the subject into sharper focus. These are Alexandre Kojève's interpretation of the end-of-history thesis and Jacques Derrida's conception of a "messianicity without messianism". Each of these figures provide important negative points of reference for Agamben throughout his discussions of time and history; even so, Agamben's critique of Kojève is somewhat less forthright than that of Derrida. The positive importance of Kojève's thought is his introduction of the notion of *désœuvrement*, or inoperativity, into philosophy in a review of the work of Raymond Queneau. This notion, which also points to the nub of the intellectual conflict between Kojève and Georges Bataille, provides Agamben with a starting point for his own construal of *désœuvrement* as centrally concerning an understanding of *potentiality*. Specifically, in *Homo Sacer* he suggests that it requires an idea of "a generic mode of potentiality that is not exhausted" in the transition of potentiality and actuality (*HS*: 62). I discuss this notion further below. But we should also recall here that potentiality is intimately associated with the problem of political sovereignty, since it is by virtue of describing the "most authentic nature" of potentiality that Aristotle bequeaths the paradigm of sovereignty to Western philosophy.

This connection brings to the fore the first element of Agamben's critique of Kojève. This is that his proposal for a homogeneous state instituted subsequent to the end of history is directly analogous to the situation of law being in force without significance (*HS*: 60). Thus Kojève's first failure is to think the end of history without the simultaneous end of the state. In Agamben's view, this approach is unequal to the task of the appropriation of historicity since this requires opening to a wholly "nonstatal and nonjuridical politics and human life" (*ME*: 112). Agamben expands on this critique in *The Open*, where he argues that in his construal of the relation of man to his animal nature post-history, Kojève fails to recognize that modern biopower turns on an increased concern for the natural life of man. That is, Kojève argues that the post-historical condition of humanity revealed in Japanese "snobbery" entails negating the " 'natural' or 'animal' given"[14] and living in accordance with purely formal principles. But this emphasis on the negation of animality (while also presupposing its survival as the support for post-historical man) condemns Kojève's thought to ignorance of the biopolitical capture of the natural life of man and, consequently, his thought remains within the horizon of the anthropological machine of modern politics. In addition to this, Agamben argues that Kojève's Hegelian view of the post-historical condition cannot give rise to a genuine understanding of the messianic, since it elides the messianic remaining time with an eschatological end of time (*TR*: 101).

But if the problem with the end-of-history thesis is that it flattens the messianic and the eschatological, Derrida's conception of a "messianicity without messianism" could be said to suffer from the reverse problem. That is, it cannot allow time to come to an end. Two central aspects of Derrida's approach to questions of end and origin throughout his *œuvre* are the inter-related emphases on deferral and the imperative of absolute futurity. These emerge in his construal of *différance* as incessant deferral of presence and origin, as well as the "ordeal of undecidability" and the notion of the *arrivant* that structures much of his later work.[15] It is overly simplistic to construe the *arrivant* and the idea of the "to-come" to which it is intimately linked as directed solely towards the future as that which is not yet present. For Derrida, the "to-come" references an event that is never exhausted in arriving or in taking place because it never fully arrives or takes place. The event of justice, for instance, is always and necessarily *à-venir*. This means that even if there is or can be an instance of its actualization, justice remains irreducibly "to-come" in so far as it remains open to absolute futurity, the promise of the future as such.[16] In relation to messianic time, the emphasis on deferral and futurity leads Derrida to posit the necessity of a "messianic without messianism".[17] In this, he attempts to strip a conception of the messianic of all specific religious traditions and "all determinable figures of the wait or expectation". Instead, the term "messianic" attempts to name a universal structure of absolute hospitality or openness to alterity (futurity), that is, a "waiting without horizon of expectation".[18] But in Agamben's view, the emphasis in deconstruction on suspension and deferral – and especially the deferral of origin and foundation – means that "deconstruction is a thwarted messianism, a suspension of the messianic" (*TR*: 102–4, 103).

This point of contrast between Agamben and Derrida is well illustrated in their differing interpretations of Franz Kafka's parable "Before the Law".[19] In Derrida's view, the key moment in this parable of the man from the country arriving before the open door of the law is the doorkeeper's response to the man's request to enter, the "not yet", or "not at the moment". Derrida suggests that this indefinitely defers the decision on whether the man from the country can pass through the door. The deferral of passage is not a direct prohibition but an interruption that delays access to the law itself, a paradoxical situation given that it is the law that also delays that access.[20] For Derrida, this suggests that the law might be understood as "a nothing that incessantly defers access to itself, thus forbidding itself in order thereby to become something or someone".[21] Further, the incessant deferral of the decision on whether the man from the country can pass through the door means that the parable is "an account of an event which arrives *at* not arriving, which manages not to happen".[22]

In Agamben's interpretation, though, the parable is not an account of an event that never happens, or that happens in not happening, but exactly the reverse: Kafka's parable describes "how something really has happened in seeming not to happen".[23] As he argues in *Homo Sacer* and elsewhere, this parable allegorizes the law as being in force without significance, and the apparent *aporias* of it express the complexity of the messianic task. For Agamben the open door of the law is analogous to the operation of the law in the ban, since it asks nothing of the man from the country and imposes nothing on him except its own suspension. The man from the country appears as a figure of the Messiah, whose task it is to fulfil the law: his behaviour is a "complicated and patient strategy" to have the door closed in order to interrupt the law's being in force without significance. For Agamben, the final line of the parable – in which the doorkeeper says "No one else could enter here, since this door was destined for you alone. Now I will go and close it" – indicates the success of the messianic event in fulfilling the Nothing of the law.

This comment on Kafka already indicates the close association that Agamben makes between the messianic and law, particularly in terms of the "fulfilment" of the law as a means of moving beyond modern nihilism understood as the condition of legal exception and abandonment. But this association and its implications are clarified in *The Time That Remains*, where Agamben argues that Paul furnishes the best way to understand the relation of messianism to law. For Agamben, Paul's reflections on faith (*pistis*) and promise (*epaggelia*) cannot be understood apart from his critique of *nomos*. What is at stake in this critique, though, is not a simple rejection of law, but a separation of its normative or prescriptive elements from its "promissive" elements, the second of which indicates that "there is something in law that constitutively exceeds the norm and is irreducible to it" (*TR*: 95). This other element of law is construed as a messianic "law of faith", which is set against the normative element of law without simply eradicating or replacing it. Significantly, Paul characterizes the relation of the law of faith to normative law with the verb *katargeo* – which Agamben posits derives from the adjective *argos*, meaning "inoperative, not-at-work (*a-ergos*), inactive", and which comes to mean to make inoperative or deactivate. Thus he suggests that "*désœuvrement*" would be a good translation for Pauline *katargein* (*TR*: 101).

The effect of the messianic law of faith, then, is not to destroy the (normative element) of law, but to render it *inoperative*: as Agamben writes, "[t]he messianic is not the destruction but the deactivation of the law, rendering the law inexecutable" (*TR*: 98). In this context, deactivation means that the potentiality or force of law is not realized or does not pass into actuality, but is instead given back to law such that the law is maintained in a state of potentiality. This condition of suspension in potentiality is what Agamben appears to mean by the fulfilment of law – the law is brought to its end in being rendered inoperative. Or,

> Only to the extent that the Messiah renders the *nomos* inoperative, that he makes the *nomos* no-longer-at-work and thus restores it to the state of potentiality, only in this way may he represent its *telos* as both end and fulfillment. The law can be brought to fulfillment only if it is first restored to the inoperativity of its power.　　(*Ibid.*)

The implication of this is that rather than being destroyed, the law is preserved by the "weak" power of the Messiah in so far as it is returned to its own potentiality, which is never exhausted in passing into actuality. Thus "Messianic *katargesis* does not merely abolish; it preserves and brings to fulfillment" (*ibid.*: 99). But this is not to say that there is no change consequent upon *nomos* being rendered inoperative. For rendering inoperative and thus fulfilling the law ultimately amounts to a progression to a "better state" (*ibid.*: 98–9). This prompts us to ask what outline of this "better state" may be discerned in Agamben's thought, and thus returns us to the notion of happiness, and moreover, to its political significance.

A politics of pure means: play, *désœuvrement* and the coming community

The notion of inoperativity and the closely related concept of *désœuvrement* or the unworked are central to Agamben's theorization of political liberation. However, this is not to suggest that he simply reiterates a political theology or politics of faith. Instead, he emphasizes the necessity of a politics that renders the current biopolitical machine inoperative through play and profanation. That is, he highlights the power of a relation to things, concepts and ultimately law itself that desacralizes and *plays* with things as a child does with toys. In this section, the concepts of play and profanation are considered in the context of Agamben's political theory, itself best understood in the formula derived from Benjamin of a politics of "pure means" that focuses on and lauds the idea of "means without end". This consideration will bring together the formulations of time, history and the messianic fulfilment of law with his vision of a "better state" elaborated in the notion of happy life and the idea of "whatever being". It will allow us to begin to assess Agamben's intervention as a theory of political liberation, especially in terms of the tools it provides for engaging with the contemporary conditions of existence such as the decline of the Westphalian nation-state system, globalized capital, and what has come to be known as the politics of difference.

Agamben's early formulation of play is proposed in *Infancy and History*, and particularly the chapter "In Playland", in which he analyses the function of rituals and play in relation to time, and claims that the revelatory characteristic of toys is to make present and tangible human temporality in itself. Agamben begins this essay by citing Collodi's description of "Playland" in *Pinocchio*, in which a population entirely composed of boys partakes in all manner of games, creating a noisy and unconstrained pandemonium of play, the effect of which is to change and accelerate time and halt the repetition and alteration of the calendar. Drawing on Benveniste's study of play and the sacred, Agamben posits that "Playland is a country whose inhabitants are busy celebrating rituals, and manipulating objects and sacred words, whose sense and purpose they have, however, forgotten . . . In play, man frees himself from sacred time and 'forgets' it in human time" (*IH*: 70). Additionally, play preserves profane objects and behaviours that otherwise no longer exist, evident in the use that children make of objects that have outlasted their functional use-value but are still taken up as toys. Thus "the toy is what belonged – *once, no longer* – to the realm of the sacred or of the practical–economic . . . the essence of the toy . . . is, then, an eminently historical thing; indeed, it is so to speak, the Historical in its pure state" (*ibid.*: 71). The toy preserves of its sacred or economic model "the human temporality that was contained therein: its pure historical essence . . . The toy is a materialization of the historicity contained in objects . . . [it] makes present and renders tangible human temporality in itself, the pure differential margin between the 'once' and the 'no longer'" (*ibid.*: 71–2).

Agamben returns to the thematic of play in his more recent work, *Profanations*. Rather than tying play to the question of time and history as in the earlier discussion, here he construes it as a means within a general strategy of resistance to the current "extreme phase" of spectacular capitalism. In the penultimate chapter of this short book, Agamben isolates profanation as a process of extracting things from the realm of the sacred and returning them to a "free use of men" (*P*: 73), such that the thing so returned is "pure, profane, free of sacred names" (*ibid.*). One of the ways that such profanation can be effectuated is in play, since "play frees and distracts humanity from the sphere of the sacred, without simply abolishing it" (*ibid.*: 76). But the impact of play is not felt solely in relation to the sacred, for as with children "who play with whatever old things fall into their hands", play can also be used to free humanity in relation to economics, law and so on. Importantly, the reference to freeing humanity does not mean simply setting these spheres aside, thereby overcoming their oppressive effects through simple destruction. Nor does it entail restoring a more natural or uncontaminated use to the things that are rendered as toys in the children's play kit. Instead, play gives onto a new use: play releases objects and ideas from the inscribed use within a given sphere and severs their instrumental attachment to an end or goal. As Agamben writes, "[t]he freed behaviour still reproduces and mimics the forms of the activity from which it has been emancipated, but, in emptying them of their sense and of any obligatory relationship to an end, it opens them and makes them available for a new use" (*ibid.*: 85–6). Given that Agamben commends play as a political task, the question to ask is what value an activity that repeats and mimics while severing the connection to an end has as a means of political liberation or resistance.

Several points can be made about the value of Agamben's intervention as a theory of political liberation. The first of these returns us to the issue of the relation of messianism and law, to consider Agamben's advocacy at various points of the idea of playing with law. We saw in *The Time That Remains* that the Messiah fulfils the law not by setting it aside or annihilating it, but by maintaining it and rendering it inoperative. Transferring this idea of inoperativity into the more profane context of the exceptional politics characteristic of biopolitical sovereignty, in *State of Exception*, Agamben similarly writes:

> One day humanity will play with law just as children play with disused objects, not in order to restore them to their canonical use but to free them from it for good. What is found after the law is not a more proper and original use value that precedes the law, but a new use that is born only after it. And use, which has been contaminated by law, must also be freed from its own value. This liberation is the task of study, or of play. And this studious play is the passage that allows us to arrive at that justice that one of Benjamin's posthumous fragments defines as a state of the world in which the world appears as a good that absolutely cannot be appropriated or made juridical. (*SE*: 64)

Thus, in this context, play allows for the profanation of law, where this is understood as the non-instrumental appropriation of law and ultimately its deactivation. The "free use" of law within play exceeds the constraints of instrumentality and yields a justice that Agamben identifies as akin to a condition in which the world can no longer be appropriated by law. Play ensures a passage to a justice that is irreducible to law – it gives rise to a new use of law that is neither simply the annihilation of law nor the constitution of a new law. It is law rendered inoperative, and as such, the gate to justice.

In both *State of Exception* and *Profanations*, Agamben draws on a comment from Benjamin in relation to the status of law in the writings of Kafka. In his essay on Kafka, Benjamin writes – in two consecutive but not obviously consistent sentences – that "The law which is studied but no longer practiced is the gate to justice" and then, immediately afterwards, "The gate to justice is study". It would be interesting to consider the superimposition of study onto law as the gate to justice in these sentences. But what is more important here is that in the quote from *State of Exception* Agamben interpellates his conception of play into this comment from Benjamin, to suggest that the deactivation of law comes about through study or play. In *Profanations*, he clarifies his point by replacing the notion of study with play to extend the notion of profanation from its direct relation to the sacred or religious to other spheres such as law. Thus he writes, "[j]ust as the *religio* that is played with but no longer observed opens the gate to use, so the powers (*potenze*) of economics, law, and politics, deactivated in play, can become the gateways to a new happiness" (*P*: 76). Hence Agamben's point concerning play is directly analogous to the role of study for Kafka, at least as Benjamin understands it: for Benjamin, the gate to justice is study; for Agamben, the gate to happiness is play.

The second point to make relates to the centrality of the notion of play within Agamben's broader formulation of a politics of "pure means". Agamben argues that as an "organ of profanation", play is in decline, and "to return to play its purely profane vocation is a political task" (*P*: 77). The particular import of this political task as it is characterized in *Profanations* is to offer a means of resistance to the conditions of the current "extreme phase" of capitalism, and most particularly to the spectacular cultural regime of consumption that is integral to it. In his classic analysis of the capitalist cultural form as spectacle, Guy Debord argues that spectacular capitalism operates through separation and division, including but not limited to the separation of image and reality, the separation of the worker from their products and the infinitesimal "parcellization" of gestures in the division of labour. For Debord, "[s]eparation is the alpha and omega of the spectacle".[24] Further, he claims that the spectacle is "basically tautological" in so far as its means are simultaneously its ends. "It is the sun that never sets over the empire of modern passivity".[25]

Without explicitly mentioning Debord at this point, Agamben similarly argues that the current extreme phase of capital is marked by separation, in which even the human body, language and sexuality are divided from themselves and placed in a separate sphere of consumption. Further, what is distinctive about this sphere is that it aims towards the impossibility of use. Agamben writes, "the capitalist religion in its extreme phase aims at creating something absolutely unprofanable" (P: 82) – that is, something that cannot be returned to the free use of man. This aim, he argues, is evident in modern consumption, tourism and the "museification" of the world. Against this impossibility of use, Agamben claims that the point of profanation is not precisely to abolish the separations of the spectacular society but to put them to a new use. He writes, "[t]o profane means not simply to abolish and erase separations but to learn to put them to a new use, to play with them . . . in order to transform them into pure means" (P: 87). Thus, in this new use, all relation to a goal or end is severed and the thing played with is free in the sense that the shape or purpose of play is not constrained by a predetermined end. It is a new use that equates to a pure means, or means without end.

This notion of pure means finds its apogee in gesture. Gestures are movements of the human body that are neither willed action (*praxis*) nor production, and as such are removed from the relation to an end or goal. Gesture does nothing but make means visible as themselves. To concretize, this is evident in tics and gestures such as tapping, rubbing or stroking one's chin or nose, touching or squeezing one's lips or pulling and twirling hair that people regularly but idiosyncratically display at academic presentations, for example. While these gestures might be read as indications of concentration, perplexity or boredom, they are not intended to mean this: they are done without purpose, often without conscious awareness at all. But just as such gestures are fleeting, so Agamben adds the caveat that playing with the separations of consumer capital is itself only temporary or episodic since "nothing . . . is as fragile and precarious as the sphere of pure means". The freedom achieved in play is inevitably recaptured such that "normal life must once again continue on its course" (P: 87).

Given Agamben's claim that "politics is the sphere of pure means, that is, of the absolute and complete gesturality of human beings" (ME: 60), we can legitimately ask how this characterization of political resistance as play and gesture relates to and, moreover, transforms the contemporary conditions of existence within globalized capital. More specifically, if capital is itself characterized by use without end, then in what way does a politics of pure means give rise to forms of liberation? Agamben's argument in this regard both repeats and complements that of an earlier text, *The Coming Community*. One of the threads of this complex and anomalous essay extends from Debord's characterization of the spectacle to argue that the modern commodification of the human body at once redeems the body from its ineffability as either biology or biography, such that it appears for the first time as "perfectly communicable, entirely illuminated" (CC: 48). However, the promise of happiness that this revelation and redemption of the body provides a glimpse of has been captured by the spectacle of capitalism and the "complete domination of the commodity form over all aspects of social life", since what was commodified was less the body than its image. The task that remains, then, is to push this process to its completion so as "to appropriate the historic transformations of human nature that capitalism wants to limit to the spectacle, to link together image and body in a space where they can no longer be separated" (ibid.: 50). Provocatively, Agamben contends that two ostensibly unlikely cultural phenomena are the "unknowing midwives" of this task: advertising and pornography.

While Agamben does not pursue this line of thought in detail in *The Coming Community*, the role of pornography as the midwife of happiness is reiterated in *Profanations*, where he suggests that pornography seeks to neutralize the profanatory potential of human erotic behaviours. Here, pornography is cast as having achieved, perhaps more than any other apparatus, "the capitalist dream of producing an unprofanable" (P: 88–9). In this light, Agamben's later characterization of pornography is less enthusiastic than previous renditions; nevertheless, the implication is that pornography itself could be put to a new use or at least could allow the eroticism otherwise captured in it to be made available for a new, freer, use. Agamben's point is obscure in this regard, but he seems to have such a new use in mind when he comments of one particular porn star, Chloe des Lysses, that her display of inexpressivity and indifference makes her face appear as a "pure means" (ibid.: 91) that thus renders the apparatus of pornography inoperative. Given the rejection in principle of the new use achieved in profanation entailing a return to a more natural use that precedes its capture in spectacle, the necessary response to pornography's capture of human eroticism cannot simply be a return to a more natural sexual expressivity. It is instead the new use achieved in absolute inexpressivity that jams the interpellative logic upon which pornography thrives.

If the inexpressive and indifferent face of a porn star can be seen as the key figure of liberation that Agamben proposes in his discussion of the potential of play and profanation, it is hard to know what one can make of this as a mode of political transformation. This is at the least a disappointing portrayal in the light of the critical analysis of biopolitical sovereignty in *Homo Sacer*. Moreover, in the absence of any further explanation from Agamben, it is not clear how repetition and mimicry of the characteristics of capitalist commodification amounts to a form of liberation rather than simply an entrenchment of them. Charming as the notion of play might be, it is not hard to imagine that the gestures of playful repetition and temporary *désœuvrement* that Agamben urges may be as empty and deadly as the regime of spectacular capitalism against which they are posed.

What is ultimately central to grasping this formulation of political liberation is the question of completion: in what sense does such a "completion" of the apparatuses of capture actually amount to a form of liberation? What, in fact, does completion mean and require in this context? It is possible to venture that the central problem in Agamben's work is exactly the issue of completion: what is it to "complete" something? Or, what is it for something to be "completed" – and not simply a task among others, but humanity itself? The importance of the issue of completion is already hinted at in *Language and Death,* where Agamben concedes that a more extensive analysis of Heidegger's *Ereignis* and Hegel's Absolute must "certainly begin with the problem of completion" (*LD*: 103), which is itself inseparable from questions of tradition and the end of history. Moreover, in so far as it is directly related to the problem of language and negativity, the question of completion is integral to social praxis. As Agamben writes, "a completed foundation for humanity" requires the elimination of the "sacrificial mythogeme and the ideas of nature and culture, of the speakable and the unspeakable, which are grounded in it . . . the *ethos*, humanity's own, is not something unspeakable or *sacer* that must remain unsaid in all praxis and human speech . . . Rather, it is social praxis itself, human speech itself, which have become transparent to themselves" (*LD*: 106).

This characterization brings us to the third and final point to make here concerning Agamben's politics of pure means, especially in relation to the text *The Coming Community.* As its title suggests, this text is ostensibly engaged with questions of community and contributes to a broader engagement with this concept, particularly by Maurice Blanchot and Jean-Luc Nancy in France, and Alphonso Lingis in the Anglo-American context. As such, it is in this text that Agamben most explicitly addresses the rethinking of community that his early analyses of language and metaphysics suggested was required. The aim of the engagement is to develop a conception of community that does not presuppose commonality or identity as a condition of belonging. In the process of this, he also engages in a long-standing debate in Western philosophy on the issue of individuation and the related distinction between identity and difference. The notion of "whatever singularity" is Agamben's response to this problem. Moreover, we can read the construal of "whatever being" as one pre-emptive articulation of the "better state" that Agamben suggests in *The Time That Remains* is achieved in the wake of the profanation of law, and associated conceptions of identity and difference. In this, the notions of "whatever being" and the coming community are perhaps Agamben's clearest articulation of a vision of a "completed humanity".

As articulated throughout *The Coming Community*, "whatever singularity" indicates a form of being that rejects any manifestation of identity or belonging, and wholly appropriates being to itself, in particular its own "being-in-language". "Whatever singularity" allows for the formation of community without the affirmation of identity or "representable condition of belonging", that is, in nothing other than the "co-belonging" of singularities itself. "Whatever being" turns around the non-identitarian unification of life with its own potentiality or "being-thus" and allows for a community of being without identity. This "life of power" (*ME*: 9) provides foundation for a new communism, in which nothing is shared except the power and possibility of life itself, and life escapes the *caesurae* and impotence to which the law has relegated it. This new communism is not strictly a utopia to be invented or found in the future, for the coming community exists now. It is a community to which all belong without claiming to belong, a community of "whatever beings" that share nothing except their own being thus in pure communicability and ontological immediacy.

The perceived political significance of this notion is evident in Agamben's claim that it is precisely the non-identitarian nature of the coming community that opposes it to the state and state political forms. Agamben argues that the community and politics of "whatever singularity" are heralded in the event of Tiananmen Square, when thousands of Chinese students, urban workers and other supporters staged an extended demonstration for about six weeks against government corruption and various reforms of the Deng Xiaoping government. What is significant about this event for Agamben is the lack of clearly articulated demands on the part of the protesters, indicating that it was not undertaken in the name of a common interest deriving from a shared identity. The lack of shared identity and interests suggests a politics of being as such, without reference to either identity or difference. In Agamben's view, the political potency of this is that ultimately the state can recognize any claim to identity but "cannot tolerate . . . that the singularities form a community without affirming an identity, that humans co-belong without any representable condition of belonging" (*CC*: 86). He concludes, then, that the coming politics will not be a struggle between states, but, instead, a struggle between the state and humanity as such, in so far as it exists in itself without expropriation in identity.

That the politics of "whatever being" are a politics beyond the end of the state indicates that "whatever being" is a name for the "better state" of existence that is realized in the wake of the fulfilment of law. The politics of "whatever being" renders the state obsolete because the state requires the inclusion of singularity in identity. Further, Agamben claims that the "hypocritical dogma of the sacredness of human life and the vacuous declarations of human rights are meant to hide" (CC: 87) exactly this obsolescence. In contrast, the politics of "whatever" involve no claims on the basis of the rights of man or citizen, nor claim a sanctity that always refers back to the figure of *homo sacer*. Instead, "whatever being" entails a mode of being in which singularity is no longer expropriated in identity and being is appropriated as such, "without being tied by any common property, by any identity" (*ibid.*: 11). And in a formulation that is strikingly similar to the premonition that one day humanity will play with law and appropriate it through a free use, Agamben suggests that "whatever being" requires the "free use of the self" that understands this as *habitus* or *ethos* – as our "second happier nature" (*ibid.*: 28–9).

The formulation of "whatever being" that Agamben presents in *The Coming Community* follows a similar logic to that which he articulates in *Stanzas* and elsewhere in relation to the notion of a pure language. In Chapters 1 and 2, we saw that what was required in Agamben's view is the accession to a language that communicates itself without remaining unsaid in what is said. Moreover, he argues that this requires the appropriation of the very barrier (/) between the sign and the signified, since this barrier acts as the point of articulation and division that ensures that meaning is the "watershed for the flow of language and the flow of revelation".[26] The conceptual linkage between "whatever being" and a pure language in which language communicates its own communicability is made explicit in the claim that

> if humans could, that is, not be-thus in this or that particular biography, but be only *the* thus, their singular exteriority and their face, then they would for the first time enter into a community without presuppositions and without subjects, into a communication without the incommunicable.[27]

But it is already implied in *The Coming Community* when Agamben argues, for instance, that "whatever being" is engendered "along a line of sparkling alternation on which common nature and singularity, potentiality and act change roles and interpenetrate" (CC: 20). As this suggests, "whatever being" is engendered on the barrier that divides and articulates being in terms of identity and difference, between the universal and the individual. "Whatever being" returns us to the fold of being itself, wherein singularity is no longer the watershed that "obliges knowledge to choose between the ineffability of the individual and the intelligibility of the universal" but is appropriated as such, "in its being *such as it is*" (*ibid.*: 1, italics in original).

Conclusion

Throughout this book, we have seen that Agamben's recent contributions to political and legal theory and to ethics are driven by and based on a complex critique of the metaphysical tendencies within Western thought. For Agamben, much Western philosophy remains tied to ways of thinking about the human that reinstitute and maintain a condition of nihilism by presupposing a non-nature at the heart of human nature. That is, by building an idea of human nature on the conception of having language, where language is founded in negativity, human nature is itself relegated to nihilism. This tendency towards a negative foundation is diagnosed most explicitly in texts such as *Language and Death*, but also underlies much of Agamben's *œuvre*. This is apparent in aesthetics, in the metaphysics of will that generates a notion of artistic production as based on the creative will and genius of the artist. In politics, this tendency is manifest in the biopolitics of the exception, wherein human life is caught within the sovereign ban and singularly exposed to death.

Agamben argues that moving beyond nihilism and the Nothing to which human nature is currently relegated requires a deep and radical rethinking of a number of aspects of Western philosophy. This includes the necessity of rethinking time and history on the basis of *kairos* (rather than *chronos*), rethinking ethics as *ethos* without reference to juridical concepts of guilt and dignity, and rethinking community without reference to identity or belonging. But most centrally, it involves an *experimentum linguae*, or a new experience of the taking place of language itself. The centrality of this aspect of the reconfiguration of Western thought is assured by the definition of the human as *zōon logon echōn*: the being that has language. This definition means that any conception of language that presupposes negativity will consequently build ideas of the human on the quicksand of negativity. In the place of such "metaphysical" conceptions of language, then, Agamben posits the urgent task of purifying the thought of language of all negativity in the forms of the ineffable or silent guarding of the un-speakable within language. That is, contemporary thought must strive to attain an understanding of the "thing itself" of language.

Agamben encapsulates the task of a new experience of the taking place of language in the idea of infancy, by which he means the mute experience of language that ontologically precedes and makes possible the appropriation of language in speech. Infancy is what the human being must undergo in order to become a subject in speech; but at the same time, speaking requires a fall from the experience of infancy into discourse. Correlative with the notion of infancy as an experience of language is Agamben's view of the necessity of returning to a pure language in which what is at stake is not this or that thing that might be said, but the sheer communicability of lan-guage itself, the very fact of language itself as the immediate mediator of the human being's location in the world. The return to or appropriation of a pure language entails a critique of conceptions of language that maintains a split between the sign and signified, and, ultimately, a reduction to the very barrier (/) that divides and articulates in such oppositions. For Agamben, the *arthron* or point of division and articulation is *logos* – and it is to return to *logos* as the fold of being that his thought ultimately aims at. It is only in returning to *logos* as the "invisible articulation" that the metaphysics that have long corrupted the thought of language as such can be overcome, along with the nihilism to which human nature is currently relegated.

While most clearly articulated in earlier works such as *Language and Death* and *Stanzas*, this understanding of the task of contemporary thought also has a significant impact on Agamben's sense of politics and ethics. This is evident, I have suggested, in the notions of "form-of-life" and "whatever singularity", which he poses as formulations for the better state that comes after the fulfilment of law. For what is at stake in Agamben's idea of politics as the sphere of pure gesture is the appropriation of the barrier (/) that divides and articulates identity/difference, life/law, fact/norm, culture/nature, human/animal or *bios/zoē* and so on. What is at issue is the appro-priation of being as such, beyond the divisions and articulations to which human being and life has been condemned within the long tradition of biopolitical sovereignty and the political theologies that underpin it. This appropriation (of the inappropriable, it should be said) is required in order to allow for a "form-of-life" or happy life in which humanity lives in the perfection of its power, in pure potentiality.

Not surprisingly, given the thoroughgoing critique of Western philo-sophy upon which it is built, this formulation of the task of contemporary thought and the politics that it opens into has significant consequences for the terms of analysis of contemporary conditions of existence. As such, the framework that Agamben is developing requires perspicacious analysis in its own right. To conclude, then, I wish very briefly to indicate possible directions for further consideration of Agamben's attempt to reorient the parameters of philosophy from the ground up. Three points are in my view particularly important. The first of these relates to the theorization of subjectivity that Agamben proposes; the second to his construal of political liberation, the notion of "form-of-life" and questions of identity and difference; and the third relates to his diagnosis of the nihilistic crisis of law and the necessity of thinking politics beyond the end of the state.

Agamben's theorization of subjectivity revolves around the constitution of subjectivity in language, specifically in the appropriation of pronouns such as "I", which, Agamben argues throughout his work, indicate the taking place of language and the simultaneous processes of subjectification and desubjectification. In this, his understanding of subjectivity is directed against the attribution of psychological properties to an individual and focuses instead on the constitution of consciousness in language. While there is ostensibly some contradiction between his anti-psychologism and the claim made in *Remnants of Auschwitz* that shame is the fundamental emotive tonality of the subject, for the most part his understanding of subjectivity is intimately tied to a theorization of pronouns as grammatical shifters. While the rejection of psychological facticity as the starting point of subjectivity is compelling, one consequence of Agamben's approach is the exclusion of materiality and embodiment from subjectivity. In fact, as he argues at one point, the phenomenal individual is necessarily set aside or expropriated in the appropriation of language that constitutes subjectivity. As I suggested at one point, then, Agamben's theorization is both anti-Cartesian and hyper-Cartesian. This poses problems for any attempt to understand the phenomenological aspects of subjectification, such as in relation to gender and sexuality. There is no obvious way to move from the constitution of consciousness in language to a discussion of the materiality of the body or the ways in which being a subject entails being embedded and constituted in relations of power and discourse.

The point to be made in relation to Agamben's theorization of political liberation, especially in relation "whatever being" and a "form-of-life" that is lived in the perfection of its own power, and questions of identity and difference, is not unrelated to this. If Agamben's construal of a better state beyond biopolitical nihilism is to be read in the manner that I have elaborated, as a return to *logos* as the very barrier that separates and divides *bios/zoē*, identity/difference, etc. through the appropriation of a "form-of-life", then significant questions can be asked about whether and how this allows us to address the differential political and social status of subjects. The formulation of "whatever being" as singularity as such, appropriated without reference to identity or difference, begs the question of what

135

significance race, gender, sexuality, class and other determinants of political subjectivity and power have within the context of global biopolitics. In other words, the formulation of "whatever being" runs two risks. First, it appears to relegate characteristics such as race and gender to the level of the ontic, thus setting them outside the ontological focus that Agamben's theorization valorizes. Secondly, in doing so, it risks abstracting too far from any recognition of the unequal distribution of the burdens of vulnerability and violence across social, economic and (geo)political spheres. If this is the case, then it is difficult to see how the formulation of biopolitical sovereignty and the production of bare life can be used as a critical diagnostic in analyses of power and subjectivity.

Thirdly, then, Agamben's formulation of a politics beyond the state risks a version of conceptual absolutism. In this view, all legal and state apparatuses, and the concepts that guide and underpin them, are seen as dangerously destructive for humanity, while the "everlasting happiness" of life beyond law is construed as wholly non-violent and unified in an appropriation without negative remainder. In rejecting all recourse to rights and law as instruments or means in a struggle for justice, Agamben's thought appears to move into a realm outside of critical intervention in unequal distributions of social, cultural political and economic resources today. While the concepts he offers for understanding the formations of power at work in current global politics seem to have some descriptive purchase – in terms of the legal exception, the ban, and bare life, for instance – the theorization of political liberation that he builds from this poses problems. For one, in its rejection of all normative concepts and corresponding emphasis on the necessity of rethinking political ontology in terms of negativity, nihilism and human nature, this account of political liberation provides very little practico-theoretical guidance for political intervention. Perhaps even more problematically, if Agamben's rejection of all normative forms of thought is to be taken seriously, then this critique would seem to obviate any justification he might have for articulating an alternative vision of a better "form-of-life". That is, one can then ask whether there is not a normative paradox or perhaps contradiction at work in the insistence on the *euporic* resolution of contemporary nihilism.

Further, Agamben's politics of pure means urges the suspension and appropriation of the interregnum between potentiality and actuality – that is, in a pure potentiality in which the corresponding privation is negated (as in the formula of not not-doing or not not-being). One of the privileged figures that Agamben draws on to illustrate this formulation is that of Melville's Bartleby, and especially his refrain of "I would prefer not to". While Bartleby may represent a form of radical potentiality in his "not not-writing", this does not seem like a particularly auspicious figuration of political transformation; nor does Agamben's emphasis on the inexpressive face in pornography in his discussion of profanation. To the extent that Agamben's theory of political liberation is ultimately based on the suspension of the passage of potentiality into action or actuality (doing or being), the worry is that his apparent philosophical radicalism passes into its opposite in the realm of politics. In other words, rather than contributing to genuinely radical political theory, his apparent radicalism passes into a kind of anti-political quietism. This is not the place to argue for this claim, but it does point to the necessity of careful analysis of the intersections of metaphysics, politics and nihilism in Agamben's conceptual web.

Notes

Chapter 1: Metaphysics: negativity, potentiality and death

1. G. W. F. Hegel, *Phenomenology of Spirit*, A. V. Miller (trans.) (Oxford: Oxford University Press, 1977), 60.
2. *Ibid.*, 65.
3. Émile Benveniste, *Problems in General Linguistics, vol. 1*, Mary Elizabeth Meek (trans.) (Coral Gables, FL: University of Miami Press, 1971), cited in *LD*: 23.
4. *Ibid.*, cited in *LD*: 23–4.
5. Hegel, *Phenomenology of Spirit*, 118.
6. The phrase is Jean-Luc Nancy's. See Jean-Luc Nancy, "Abandoned Being", in *The Birth to Presence* (Stanford, CA: Stanford University Press, 1993), 47.
7. See Martin Heidegger, "Introduction To 'What Is Metaphyics?'", in *Pathmarks*, William McNeill (ed.) (Cambridge: Cambridge University Press, 1998), 277–80.
8. Walter Benjamin, "On the Program of the Coming Philosophy", in *Selected Writings, Volume 1, 1913–1926*, Marcus Bullock & Michael W. Jennings (eds) (Cambridge, MA: Harvard University Press, 1996), 108; see also "On Perception" in the same volume, 93–6.
9. Benjamin, "The Coming Philosophy", 104.
10. *Ibid.*
11. *Ibid.*, 105.
12. The Italian term *esperienza* derives from the same Latin root.
13. Martin Heidegger, "The Nature of Language", in *On the Way to Language*, Peter D. Hertz (trans.) (New York: HarperCollins, 1982), 57.
14. While "synderesis" is generally understood to indicate remorse, guilt or a prick of conscience, Agamben counters that it is a "technical term used in Neoplatonic mysticism of the Middle Ages and the Renaissance to designate the highest and most delicate area of the soul" which is "in direct communication with the supersensory, and has never been corrupted by original sin". He cites the Arab mystic, Al-Hallaj as providing the definitive articulation of the "transcendental experience" at the heart of the *cogito* or I: "I am *I* and the attributes are no more; I am *I* and the qualifications are no more . . . I am the pure subject of the verb" (*IH*: 30).
15. Aristotle, *Metaphysics, Books I–IX*, Hugh Tredennick (trans.), Loeb Classical Library (Cambridge, MA: Harvard University Press, 2003), 461 (1046a 30–35).
16. *Ibid.*, 461 (1050ba 5–10).
17. *Ibid.*, 439 (1047a 20–25).

139

18. Daniel Heller-Roazen, "Editor's Introduction: 'To Read What Was Never Written'," in *Potentialities: Collected Essays in Philosophy*, Daniel Heller-Roazen (ed. & trans.) (Stanford, CA: Stanford University Press, 1999), 18.
19. See also Agamben, "Bartleby, or on Contingency", in *Potentialities*.
20. Benjamin, cited in Agamben, "Bartleby", 268.
21. Rendering the political implications of this in terms of the characteristic separation of political and natural life, Agamben suggests that "the child is a paradigm of a life that is absolutely inseparable from its form, an absolute form-of-life [*forma-di-vita*] without remainder". But this is not because the life of the child is somehow mysterious or impenetrable, but rather because "it adheres so closely to its physiological life that it becomes indiscernible from it". Troublingly, Agamben suggests that in being tied more closely to physiological conditions, the life of the child is akin to the life of a woman.
22. For a further discussion of potentiality and language, see Heller-Roazen, "Editor's Introduction: 'To Read What Was Never Written'."

Chapter 2: Aesthetics: language, representation and the object

1. Agamben's formulation of this argument is somewhat idiosyncratic and involves running together reason, word and world. He also states: "The fact that I speak and that someone listens implies the existence of nothing – other than language." But this is a restricted interpretation, since the existence of some thing that speaks and another that listens is already presupposed in this formulation. This is to say nothing about the presupposition that "I" speak – thus raising a logical problem that is close to the circularity inherent in Descartes's *cogito ergo sum*. Agamben's formulation and interpretation here go directly to the question of alterity that I discuss further in the chapter on ethics.
2. Wittgenstein, *Philosophical Investigations*, §309; cited in Agamben, "The Idea of Language", 46.
3. Walter Benjamin, "The Task of the Translator", in *Walter Benjamin: Selected Writings, Volume 1, 1913–1926*, 262.
4. However, the engagement between Agamben and Derrida is largely one-sided. Whereas Agamben dedicates several essays to Derrida – including the essay discussed earlier entitled "The Thing Itself" – and most if not all of his books contain a critical reference to Derrida or deconstruction, Derrida's contribution to the debate was considerably less. He did not respond to the provocations from Agamben, except in the posthumously published book *Rogues*, in which he is sharply critical of Agamben's interpretation of Aristotle's political theory and the resulting formulation of biopolitical sovereignty.
5. Jacques Derrida, *Dissemination*, B. Johnson (trans.) (Chicago, IL: University of Chicago Press, 1981).
6. Though he ultimately rejects this, arguing that *différance* is a not a concept but "the possibility of conceptuality, of a conceptual process and system in general" (Jacques Derrida, *Margins of Philosophy*, Alan Bass (trans.) (Chicago, IL: University of Chicago Press, 1982), 11).
7. *Ibid.*, 9.
8. *Ibid.*, 7.
9. *Ibid.*, 15; italics added.
10. This discussion of taste should be read in the light of the comment from Walter Benjamin that the task of the critic is to investigate why the doctrine of taste is now obsolete. Walter Benjamin, "The Task of the Critic", in *Selected Writings Volume 2, Part 2, 1931–1934*, Michael W. Jennings, Howard Eiland & Gary Smith (eds) (Cambridge, MA: Harvard University Press, 1999), 548.

11. Hegel, cited in Agamben, *Man Without Content*, 36.
12. See Hannah Arendt, *The Human Condition*, 2nd edn (Chicago, IL: University of Chicago Press, 1998).

Chapter 3: Politics: biopolitics, sovereignty and nihilism

1. Michel Foucault, *The History of Sexuality, Volume 1: An Introduction*, Richard Hurley (trans.) (London: Penguin, 1981), 136.
2. *Ibid.*, 141–2.
3. *Ibid.*, 142.
4. *Ibid.*, 143.
5. Carl Schmitt, *Political Theology: Four Chapters on the Concept of Sovereignty*, George Schwab (trans.) (Cambridge, MA: MIT Press, 1985), 5.
6. *Ibid.*, 13.
7. Agamben, *Homo Sacer*, 25. For a further discussion of exemplarity within Agamben's work, see Steven D. DeCaroli, "Visibility and History: Giorgio Agamben and the Exemplary", *Philosophy Today* 45(2001), 9–17.
8. J.-L. Nancy, "Abandoned Being", in *The Birth to Presence* (Stanford, CA: Stanford University Press), 43–4.
9. Agamben, *Homo Sacer*, 51; it is important to note here that Agamben's critique of law is not simply targeted at positive law, but at "the entire text of tradition in its regulative form, whether the Jewish Torah or the Islamic Shariah, Christian dogma or the profane *nomos*" (*ibid.*). This recognition is important not only for measuring the stakes of Agamben's criticism, but also for understanding the conceptual linkage – beyond the thematic of biopolitics – between *Homo Sacer* and *Remnants of Auschwitz*.
10. The key parable of Kafka for Agamben is "Before the Law", in which a man from the country presents himself before the doorkeeper who refuses to let him enter through the door (of the law). The man from the country waits indefinitely, only to be told towards the end of his life that the door was meant for him alone. A more extensive discussion of this parable is available in Agamben, "The Messiah and the Sovereign".
11. See the discussion of Benjamin in Agamben, *Homo Sacer*, 53–6. Also compare Agamben's discussion of Kafka in the same section of *Homo Sacer*.
12. Agamben is not at all sensitive to the gendered dimension of the exclusion of natural life from the realm of the political in his treatment of biopolitics, although feminists have long argued that the association of femininity with natural, biological life is a consistent element of the Western political and cultural imaginary.
13. See especially Foucault, *History of Sexuality, Vol. 1*, 135–43.
14. Walter Benjamin, "On the Concept of History", in *Selected Writings, Volume 4, 1938–1940*, Howard Eiland & Michael W. Jennings (eds) (Cambridge, MA: Harvard University Press, 2003), 392.
15. Walter Benjamin, "Critique of Violence", in *Selected Writings, Volume 1, 1913–1926*, 236–52.
16. For example, see João Biehl, "Vita: Life in a Zone of Social Abandonment", *Social Text* 19(3) (2001); Diane Enns, "Bare Life and the Occupied Body", *Theory & Event* 7(3) (2004); Fiona Jenkins, "Bare Life: Asylum-Seekers, Australian Politics and Agamben's Critique of Violence", *Australian Journal of Human Rights* 10(1) (2004); Agamben, *Homo Sacer*, 185–6.
17. For further discussion of the role of "bare life" in Agamben's political theory, see Andrew Norris, "Giorgio Agamben and the Politics of the Living Dead", *Diacritics* 30(4) (2000).
18. See Walter Benjamin, "Critique of Violence", 251.

19. The ambiguation between biological or nutritive life and bare life is especially evident in this essay.
20. Gilles Deleuze, "Immanence: A Life", in *Pure Immanence: Essays on a Life* (New York: Urzone, 2001), 31.
21. *Ibid.*, 28; see also Gilles Deleuze, "L'immanence: Une Vie . . .", *Philosophie* 47, 1 September 1995, where the relevant phrase is "quelque chose de doux le penetrer" (5).
22. Agamben, "Absolute Immanence", 229; see also Agamben, "L'immanza Assoluta", *aut aut* 276, novembre-dicembre 1996, 46.
23. Antonio Negri, *Insurgencies: Constituent Power and the Modern State*, Maurizia Boscagli (trans.) (Minneapolis, MN: University of Minnesota Press, 1999), 21–2. See also Casarino & Negri, "It's a Powerful Life: A Conversation in Contemporary Philosophy", *Cultural Critique* 57 (2004), 177–9, for Negri's response to Agamben's critique in *Homo Sacer* and a further discussion of their theoretical differences on the issue of potentiality.
24. Negri, *Insurgences*, 332.
25. Casarino & Negri, "It's a Powerful Life", 169.
26. Michael Hardt & Antonio Negri, *Empire* (Cambridge, MA: Harvard University Press, 2000), 366–7.
27. *Ibid.*, 366; Michael Hardt & Thomas L. Dumm, "Sovereignty, Multitudes, Absolute Democracy: A Discussion between Michael Hardt and Thomas Dumm About Hardt and Negri's *Empire*", *Theory & Event* 4(3) (2000), §16.
28. Agamben, *Homo Sacer*, 44; see also Negri, *Insurgences*; Michael Hardt & Antonio Negri, *Labor of Dionysus: A Critique of the State-Form* (Minneapolis, MN: University of Minnesota Press, 1994).
29. Agamben, *Homo Sacer*, 43. This claim is made in the context of a critique of Antonio Negri's dis-identification of sovereign and constitutive power on the basis that while constitutive power is "the punctual determination that opens a horizon, the radical enacting of something that did not exist before and whose conditions of existence stipulate that the creative act cannot lose its characteristics in creating", sovereignty "arises as the establishment – and therefore the end – of constituting power, as the consumption of the freedom brought by constituting power" (Negri, cited in Agamben, *Homo Sacer*, 43).
30. But see the extensive debates about Foucault's conception of the body and its role in resistance in feminist theory. The phrase "economy of bodies and pleasures" is from Foucault, *History of Sexuality, Vol. 1*, 159.
31. *Ibid.*, 144.
32. *Ibid.*, 95–6.
33. See also Thomas Carl Wall, *Radical Passivity: Levinas, Blanchot and Agamben* (Albany, NY: SUNY Press, 1999), 115–62. As Wall and others note, the key characteristic of Agamben's formulation of the coming community is that the "community of whatever" is a community that has never been: it is not a nostalgic return to *Gemeinschaft*, or an identitarian conception of community, but a notion of community predicated on the pure immanence of "whatever" beyond identity and all relation. See the discussion of this in Chapter 5.

Chapter 4: Ethics: testimony, responsibility and the witness

1. "Primo Levi", cited in Agamben, *Remnants of Auschwitz: The Witness and the Archive*, Daniel Heller-Roazen (trans.) (New York: Zone Books, 1999), 44.
2. Zygmunt Bauman, *Modernity and the Holocaust* (Cambridge: Polity, 1989).

3. Nikolas Rose, *The Politics of Life Itself: Biomedicine, Power and Subjectivity in the Twenty-First Century* (Princeton, NJ: Princeton University Press, 2007), 58–9, 69–70.
4. Ernesto Laclau, "Bare Life or Social Indeterminacy?", in *Giorgio Agamben: Sovereignty and Life*, Matthew Calarco & Steven D. DeCaroli (eds) (Stanford, CA: Stanford University Press, 2007), 22.
5. Bauman, *Modernity and the Holocaust*, 13.
6. Arendt, *The Human Condition*, 63.
7. It is worth noting that in the course of this essay Agamben refers to a "Kandellam", whom he suggests was close to Foucault. This is presumably an error of transcription and the reference should be to Georges Canguilhem.
8. Michel Foucault, *Discipline and Punish: The Birth of the Prison*, Alan Sheridan (trans.) (London: Penguin, 1979), 205, 208.
9. See Michel Foucault, "Nietzsche, Genealogy, History", in *Aesthetics, Method and Epistemology: The Essential Works of Michel Foucault 1954–1984, Volume Two*, James Faubion (ed.) (London: Penguin, 1994).
10. Paul Patton, "Agamben and Foucault on Biopower and Biopolitics", in *Giorgio Agamben: Sovereignty and Life*, 18.
11. Foucault, *History of Sexuality, Vol. 1*, 100–102.
12. Primo Levi, *The Drowned and the Saved*, R. Rosenthal (trans.) (London: Abacus, 1988), 63–4; cited in Agamben, *Remnants of Auschwitz*, 33; see also 82.
13. Foucault, *History of Sexuality, Vol. 1*, 138.
14. This idea is drawn from Emmanuel Lévinas, *On Escape*, introduced and annotated by Jacques Rolland, Bettina Bergo (trans.) (Stanford, CA: Stanford University Press, 2003), 63–5.
15. Hannah Arendt, *Imperialism: Part Two of the Origins of Totalitarianism* (Orlando, FL: Harcourt, Brace & Co., 1958), 177.
16. Michel Foucault, "Confronting Governments: Human Rights" (1984) in *Power: Essential Works of Foucault, 1954–1984, Vol. 3*, James D. Faubion (ed.), Robert Hurley & others (trans.) (New York: New Press, 2000), 474–5.
17. Michel Foucault, "Two Lectures", in *Power/Knowledge: Selected Interviews and Other Writings 1972–1977*, Colin Gordon (ed.) (New York: Pantheon, 1980), 108.
18. See Wall, *Radical Passivity*.
19. On the question of intersubjectivity and relationality in testimony, see Kelly Oliver, *Witnessing: Beyond Recognition* (Minneapolis, MN: University of Minnesota Press, 2001).
20. On "being-with", see, in particular, Jean-Luc Nancy, *The Inoperative Community*, P. Connor (ed.), P. Connor & others (trans.) (Minneapolis, MN: University of Minnesota Press, 1991); Jean-Luc Nancy, "Of Being Singular Plural", in *Being Singular Plural*, R. D. Richardson & A. E. Byrne (trans.) (Stanford, CA: Stanford University Press, 2000), 1–100; Jean-Luc Nancy, "Of Being-in-Common", in *Community at Loose Ends*, Miami Theory Collective (eds) (Minneapolis, MN: University of Minnesota Press, 1991), 1–12.

Chapter 5: Messianism: time, happiness and completed humanity

1. Walter Benjamin, "Paralipomena To 'On the Concept of History'", in *Selected Writings, Volume 4, 1938–1940*, Howard Eiland & Michael W. Jennings (eds) (Cambridge, MA: Harvard University Press, 2003), 402.
2. In this and other ways, there is at most a *pluripotency* – not totipotency – at issue in regard to the human infant.

3. Martin Heidegger, "Letter On 'Humanism'", in *Basic Writings: From* Being and Time (1927) *to* The Task of Thinking (1964), 2nd revised and expanded edn, David Farrell Krell (ed.) (New York: HarperCollins, 1993), 217–65. In this paragraph, further page references to this work are given in parenthesis.
4. Benjamin, "One Way Street", 482.
5. Jacques Derrida, *Rogues: Two Essays on Reason*, Pascale-Anne Brault & Michael Naas (trans.) (Stanford, CA: Stanford University Press, 2005), 24.
6. Adriana Cavarero, "Equality and Sexual Difference: Amnesia in Political Thought", in *Beyond Equality and Difference: Citizenship, Feminist Politics and Female Subjectivity*, G. Bock & S. James (eds) (New York: Routledge, 1992), 32–47.
7. Walter Benjamin, "Theological–Political Fragment", in *Selected Writings Volume 3, 1935–1938*, Howard Eiland & Michael W. Jennings (eds) (Cambridge, MA: Harvard University Press, 2002), 305.
8. *Ibid.*, 305, 306.
9. *Ibid.*, 305; Agamben, "Benjamin and the Demonic: Happiness and Historical Redemption", in *Potentialities*, 154.
10. Benjamin, "On the Concept of History", 395.
11. Benjamin, "Paralipomena", 402.
12. Benjamin, "On the Concept of History", 391. In this paragraph, further page references to this work are given in parentheses.
13. Benjamin, "On the Concept of History", 397; Agamben, *Time That Remains*, 71.
14. Kojève, cited in Agamben, *The Open*, 11; Alexandre Kojève, *Introduction to the Reading of Hegel*, Allan Bloom (ed.), James H. Nichols Jnr (trans.), assembled by Raymond Queneau (New York: Basic Books, 1969), 158–62.
15. For a more extensive discussion of origin and deferral in Derrida's work see Paola Marrati, *Genesis and Trace: Derrida Reading Husserl and Heidegger*, Simon Sparks (trans.) (Stanford, CA: Stanford University Press, 2005).
16. Or to bring out the point of contrast in another way, we can rewrite this conception of futurity into the problem of potentiality. As I discussed in Chapter 1, key to Agamben's construal of potentiality is the appropriation and maintenance of impotentiality in the passage to actuality. For Derrida, one might venture that what is important is the capacity of that which is potential to maintain itself in its own impotentiality and thereby *not* (wholly) pass into actuality.
17. Jacques Derrida, *Specters of Marx: The State of the Debt, the Work of Mourning, and the New International*, Peggy Kamuf (trans.) (New York: Routledge, 1994), passim; see also John D. Caputo (ed.), *Deconstruction in a Nutshell: A Conversation with Jacques Derrida* (New York: Fordham University Press, 1997).
18. Derrida, *Specters of Marx*, 168.
19. Franz Kafka, "Before the Law", in *The Collected Short Stories*, Nahum N. Glatzer (ed.) (London: Penguin, 1988).
20. Jacques Derrida, "Before the Law", in *Acts of Literature*, Derek Attridge (ed.) (New York: Routledge, 1992), 205.
21. *Ibid.*, 208.
22. *Ibid.*, 210; emphasis in original.
23. Agamben, "Messiah and the Sovereign", 174; see also Agamben, *Homo Sacer*, 49–58.
24. Guy Debord, *Society of the Spectacle*, Donald Nicholson Smith (trans.) (New York: Zone Books, 1995), §25, 20.
25. *Ibid.*, §13, 15.
26. The phrase is from Benjamin, "Task of the Translator", 262.
27. Agamben, *Coming Community*, 65. Note also that the idea of singularity exposed without any particular biography is a critique of Hannah Arendt's formulation of singularity in *The Human Condition*, in her discussion of the exposure of who and what someone is in biography. See Arendt, *The Human Condition*, 175–88.

Chronology of major works

Italian text	Year	English translation	Year
Stanze: La parola e il fantasma nella cultura occidentale	1977	*Stanzas: Word and Phantasm in Western Culture*	1993
Infanzia e storia	1978	*Infancy and History*	1993
Il linguaggio e la morte: un seminario sul luogo della negaivita	1982	*Language and Death: The Place of Negativity*	1991
Idea della Prosa	1985	*Idea of Prose*	1995
La communita che viene	1990	*The Coming Community*	1993
L'uomo senza contenuto	1970/ 1994	*The Man Without Content*	1999
Categorie Italiane: studi di poetica	1996	*The End of the Poem: Studies in Poetics*	1999
Homo Sacer: Il potere sovrana e la nuda vita	1995	*Homo Sacer: Sovereign Power and Bare Life*	1998
Essays published separately	1983–96	*Potentialities*	1999
Mezza sensa fine	1996	*Means without End: Notes on Politics*	2000
Quel che resta di Auschwitz	1998	*Remnants of Auschwitz: The Witness and the Archive*	1999
Il tempo che resta. Un commento alla Lettera ai Romani	2000	*The Time That Remains: A Commentary on the Letter to the Romans*	2005
L'aperto: L'uomo e l'animale	2002	*The Open: Man and Animal*	2004
Stato di eccezione	2003	*State of Exception*	2005
Profanazioni	2005	*Profanations*	2007

Bibliography

Works by Giorgio Agamben

Agamben, G. 1991. *Language and Death: The Place of Negativity*, Karen E. Pinkus & Michael Hardt (trans.). Minneapolis, MN: University of Minnesota Press.

Agamben, G. 1993. *Infancy and History: Essays on the Destruction of Experience*, Liz Heron (trans.). London: Verso.

Agamben, G. 1993. *Stanzas: Word and Phantasm in Western Culture*, Ronald L. Martinez (trans.). Minneapolis, MN: University of Minnesota Press.

Agamben, G. 1993. *The Coming Community*, Michael Hardt (trans.). Minneapolis, MN: University of Minnesota Press.

Agamben, G. 1995. *Idea of Prose*, Michael Sullivan & Sam Whitsitt (trans.). Albany, NY: SUNY Press.

Agamben, G. 1996. "L'immanza Assoluta", *aut aut* 276, no. novembre–dicembre: 39–57.

Agamben, G. 1998. *Homo Sacer: Sovereign Power and Bare Life*, Daniel Heller-Roazen (trans.). Stanford, CA: Stanford University Press.

Agamben, G. 1999. "Bartleby, or on Contingency". In *Potentialities: Collected Essays in Philosophy*, Daniel Heller-Roazen (ed.), 243–71. Stanford, CA: Stanford University Press.

Agamben, G. 1999. "Benjamin and the Demonic: Happiness and Historical Redemption". In *Potentialities: Collected Essays in Philosophy*, Daniel Heller-Roazen (ed.), 138–59. Stanford, CA: Stanford University Press.

Agamben, G. 1999. "Kommerell, or On Gesture". In *Potentialities: Collected Essays in Philosophy*, Daniel Heller-Roazen (ed.), 77–85. Stanford, CA: Stanford University Press.

Agamben, G. 1999. "Language and History". In *Potentialities: Collected Essays in Philosophy*, Daniel Heller-Roazen (ed.), 48–61. Stanford, CA: Stanford University Press.

Agamben, G. 1999. "On Potentiality". In *Potentialities: Collected Essays in Philosophy*, Daniel Heller-Roazen (ed.), 177–84. Stanford, CA: Stanford University Press.

Agamben, G. 1999. "*Pardes*: The Writing of Potentiality". In *Potentialities: Collected Essays in Philosophy*, Daniel Heller-Roazen (ed.), 205–19. Stanford, CA: Stanford University Press.

Agamben, G. 1999. *Potentialities: Collected Essays in Philosophy*, Daniel Heller-Roazen (ed.). Stanford, CA: Stanford University Press.

Agamben, G. 1999. *Remnants of Auschwitz: The Witness and the Archive*, Daniel Heller-Roazen (trans.). New York: Zone Books.

Agamben, G. 1999. *The End of the Poem: Studies in Poetics*, Daniel Heller-Roazen (trans.). Stanford, CA: Stanford University Press.

Agamben, G. 1999. *The Man Without Content*, Georgia Albert (trans.). Stanford, CA: Stanford University Press.

Agamben, G. 1999. "The Messiah and the Sovereign: The Problem of Law in Walter Benjamin". In *Potentialities: Collected Essays in Philosophy*, Daniel Heller-Roazen (ed.), 160–74. Stanford, CA: Stanford University Press.

Agamben, G. 2000. *Means without End: Notes on Politics*, Cesare Casarino & Vincenzo Binetti (trans.). Minneapolis, MN: University of Minnesota Press.

Agamben, G. 2002. "What Is a Paradigm?" http://www.egs.edu/faculty/agamben/agamben-what-is-a-paradigm-2002.html.

Agamben, G. 2004. *The Open: Man and Animal*, Kevin Attell (trans.). Stanford, CA: Stanford University Press.

Agamben, G. 2005. *State of Exception*, Kevin Attell (trans.). Chicago, IL: University of Chicago Press.

Agamben, G. 2005. *The Time That Remains: A Commentary on the Letter to the Romans*, Patricia Daley (trans.). Stanford, CA: Stanford University Press.

Agamben, G. 2007. *Profanations*, Jeff Fort (trans.). New York: Zone Books.

Agamben, G. 1999. "Absolute Immanence". In *Potentialities: Collected Essays in Philosophy*, Daniel Heller-Roazen (ed.), 220–39. Stanford, CA: Stanford University Press.

Agamben, G. 1999. "The Thing Itself". In *Potentialities: Collected Essays in Philosophy*, Daniel Heller-Roazen (ed.), 27–38. Stanford, CA: Stanford University Press.

Agamben, G. 2001. "For a Philosophy of Infancy", *Public*, http://www.yorku.ca/public/public/backissu/v21_1.html.

Other works

Arendt, H. 1958. *Imperialism: Part Two of the Origins of Totalitarianism*. Orlando, FL: Harcourt, Brace & Co.

Arendt, H. 1998. *The Human Condition*, 2nd edn. Chicago, IL: University of Chicago Press.

Aristotle. 2003. *Metaphysics, Books I–IX*, Hugh Tredennick (trans.), Loeb Classical Library. Cambridge, MA: Harvard University Press.

Bauman, Z. 1989. *Modernity and the Holocaust*. Cambridge: Polity.

Benjamin, W. 1996. "Critique of Violence". In *Selected Writings, Volume 1, 1913–1926*, Marcus Bullock & Michael W. Jennings (eds), Edmund Jephcott (trans.), 236–52. Cambridge, MA: Harvard University Press.

Benjamin, W. 1996. "On Perception". In *Selected Writings, Volume 1, 1913–1926*, Marcus Bullock & Michael W. Jennings (eds), Edmund Jephcott (trans.), 93–6. Cambridge, MA: Harvard University Press.

Benjamin, W. 1996. "On the Program of the Coming Philosophy". In *Selected Writings, Volume 1, 1913–1926*, Marcus Bullock & Michael W. Jennings (eds), Mark Rutter (trans.), 100–10. Cambridge, MA: Harvard University Press.

Benjamin, W. 1996. "One Way Street." In *Selected Writings, Volume 1, 1913–1926*, Marcus Bullock & Michael W. Jennings (eds), Edmund Jephcott (trans.), 448–88. Cambridge, MA: Harvard University Press.

Benjamin, W. 1996. "The Task of the Translator". In *Walter Benjamin: Selected Writings, Volume 1, 1913–1926*, Marcus Bullock & Michael W. Jennings (eds), Harry Zohn (trans.), 253–63. Cambridge, MA: Harvard University Press.

Benjamin, W. 1999. "The Task of the Critic". In *Selected Writings, Volume 2, Part 2, 1931–1934*, Michael W. Jennings, Howard Eiland & Gary Smith (eds), Rodney Livingstone (trans.), 548–9. Cambridge, MA: Harvard University Press.

Benjamin, W. 2002. "Theological–Political Fragment". In *Selected Writings, Volume 3, 1935–1938*, Howard Eiland & Michael W. Jennings (eds), Edmund Jephcott (trans.), 305–6. Cambridge, MA: Harvard University Press.

Benjamin, W. 2003. "On the Concept of History". In *Selected Writings, Volume 4, 1938–1940*, Howard Eiland & Michael W. Jennings (eds), Harry Zohn (trans.), 389–400. Cambridge, MA: Harvard University Press.

Benjamin, W. 2003. "Paralipomena To 'On the Concept of History'". In *Selected Writings, Volume 4, 1938–1940*, Howard Eiland & Michael W. Jennings (eds), Edmund Jephcott & Howard Eiland (trans.), 401–11. Cambridge, MA: Harvard University Press.

Benveniste, É. 1971. *Problems in General Linguistics, Volume 1*, Mary Elizabeth Meek (trans.). Coral Gables, FL: University of Miami Press.

Biehl, J. 2001. "Vita: Life in a Zone of Social Abandonment", *Social Text* 19(3), 131–49.

Calarco, M. & DeCaroli, S. D. (eds) 2007. *Georgio Agamben: Sovereignty and Life*. Stanford, CA: Stanford University Press.

Caputo, J. D. (ed.) 1997. *Deconstruction in a Nutshell: A Conversation with Jacques Derrida*. New York: Fordham University Press.

Casarino, C. & Negri, A. 2004. "It's a Powerful Life: A Conversation in Contemporary Philosophy", *Cultural Critique* 57, 151–83.

DeCaroli, S. D. 2001. "Visibility and History: Giorgio Agamben and the Exemplary", *Philosophy Today* 45, 9–17.

Debord, G. 1995. *The Society of the Spectacle*, Donald Nicholson Smith (trans.). New York: Zone Books.

Deleuze, G. 1995. "L'immanence: Une Vie . . .", *Philosophie* 47, 1 September, 3–7.

Deleuze, G. 2001. "Immanence: A Life". In *Pure Immanence: Essays on a Life*, Introduction by John Rajchman, Anne Boyman (trans.), 25–33. New York: Urzone.

Derrida, J. 1981. *Dissemination*, B. Johnson (trans.). Chicago, IL: University of Chicago Press.

Derrida, J. 1982. *Margins of Philosophy*, Alan Bass (trans.). Chicago, IL: University of Chicago Press.

Derrida, J. 1992. "Before the Law". In *Acts of Literature*, Derek Attridge (ed.), 181–220. New York: Routledge.

Derrida, J. 1994. *Specters of Marx: The State of the Debt, the Work of Mourning, and the New International*, Peggy Kamuf (trans.). New York: Routledge.

Derrida, J. 2005. *Rogues: Two Essays on Reason*, Pascale-Anne Brault & Michael Naas (trans.). Stanford, CA: Stanford University Press.

Enns, D. 2004. "Bare Life and the Occupied Body", *Theory & Event* 7(3).

Foucault, M. 1979. *Discipline and Punish: The Birth of the Prison*, Alan Sheridan (trans.). London: Penguin.

Foucault, M. 1980. "Two Lectures". In *Power/Knowledge: Selected Interviews and Other Writings 1972–1977*, Colin Gordon (ed.), 78–108. New York: Pantheon.

Foucault, M. 1981. *The History of Sexuality, Volume 1: An Introduction*, Richard Hurley (trans.). London: Penguin.

Foucault, M. 1984. "Confronting Governments: Human Rights". In *Power: Essential Works of Foucault, 1954–1984*, vol. 3, James D. Faubion (ed.), Robert Hurley & others (trans.), 474–5. New York: New Press, 2000.

Foucault, M. 1994. "Nietzsche, Genealogy, History". In *Aesthetics, Method and Epistemology: The Essential Works of Michel Foucault 1954–1984, Volume Two*, James Faubion (ed.), 369–91. London: Penguin.

Hardt, M. & Dumm, Thomas L. 2000. "Sovereignty, Multitudes, Absolute Democracy: A Discussion between Michael Hardt and Thomas Dumm About Hardt and Negri's *Empire*", *Theory & Event* 4(3).

149

Hardt, M. & Negri, A. 1994. *Labor of Dionysis: A Critique of the State-Form*. Minneapolis, MN: University of Minnesota Press.

Hardt, M. & Negri, A. 2000. *Empire*. Cambridge, MA: Harvard University Press.

Hegel, G. W. F. 1977. *Phenomenology of Spirit*, A. V. Miller (trans.). Oxford: Oxford University Press.

Heidegger, M. 1982. "The Nature of Language". In *On the Way to Language*, Peter D. Hertz (trans.), 57–108. New York: HarperCollins.

Heidegger, M. 1998. "Introduction To 'What Is Metaphysics?'" In *Pathmarks*, William McNeill (ed.), Walter Kaufman (trans.), 277–90. Cambridge: Cambridge University Press.

Heidegger, M. 1993. "Letter On 'Humanism'". In *Basic Writings: From* Being and Time (1927) *to* The Task of Thinking (1964), 2nd revised and expanded edn, David Farrell Krell (ed.). New York: HarperCollins.

Heller-Roazen, D. 1999. "Editor's Introduction: 'To Read What Was Never Written'". In *Potentialities: Collected Essays in Philosophy*, Daniel Heller-Roazen (ed.), 1–23. Stanford, CA: Stanford University Press.

Jenkins, F. 2004. "Bare Life: Asylum-Seekers, Australian Politics and Agamben's Critique of Violence", *Australian Journal of Human Rights* 10(1), 79–95.

Kafka, F. 1988. "Before the Law". In *The Collected Short Stories*, Nahum N. Glatzer (ed.), Willa & Edmund Muir (trans.), 3–4. London: Penguin.

Kojève, A. 1969. *Introduction to the Reading of Hegel*, Allan Bloom (ed.), James H. Nichols Jnr. (trans.), assembled by Raymond Queneau. New York: Basic Books.

Laclau, E. 2007. "Bare Life or Social Indeterminacy?" In *Giorgio Agamben: Sovereignty and Life*, Matthew Calarco & Steven D. DeCaroli (eds), 11–22. Stanford, CA: Stanford University Press.

Lévinas, Emmanuel. 2003. *On Escape*, Introduced and annotated by Jacques Rolland, Bettina Bergo (trans.). Stanford, CA: Stanford University Press.

Levi, Primo. 1988. *The Drowned and the Saved*, R. Rosenthal (trans.). London: Abacus.

Marrati, P. 2005. *Genesis and Trace: Derrida Reading Husserl and Heidegger*, Simon Sparks (trans.). Stanford, CA: Stanford University Press.

Nancy, J.-L. 1991. *The Inoperative Community*, P. Connor (ed.), P. Connor & others (trans.). Minneapolis, MN: University of Minnesota Press.

Nancy, J.-L. 1991. "Of Being-in-Common". In *Community at Loose Ends*, Miami Theory Collective (eds). Minneapolis, MN: University of Minnesota Press.

Nancy, J.-L. 1993. "Abandoned Being". In *The Birth to Presence*, Brian Holmes & others (trans.), 36–47. Stanford, CA: Stanford University Press.

Nancy, J.-L. 2000. "Of Being Singular Plural". In *Being Singular Plural*, R. D. Richardson & A. E. Byrne (trans.). Stanford, CA: Stanford University Press.

Negri, A. 1999. *Insurgencies: Constituent Power and the Modern State*, Maurizia Boscagli (trans.). Minneapolis, MN: University of Minnesota Press.

Norris, A. 2000. "Giorgio Agamben and the Politics of the Living Dead", *Diacritics* 30(4), 38–58.

Oliver, K. 2001. *Witnessing: Beyond Recognition*. Minneapolis, MN: University of Minnesota Press.

Patton, P. 2007. "Agamben and Foucault on Biopower and Biopolitics". In *Giorgio Agamben: Sovereignty and Life*, Matthew Calarco & Steven D. DeCaroli (eds), 203–18. Stanford, CA: Stanford University Press.

Rose, N. 2007. *The Politics of Life Itself: Biomedicine, Power and Subjectivity in the Twenty-First Century*. Princeton, NJ: Princeton University Press.

Schmitt, C. 1985. *Political Theology: Four Chapters on the Concept of Sovereignty*, George Schwab (trans.). Cambridge, MA: MIT Press.

Wall, T. C. 1999. *Radical Passivity: Lévinas, Blanchot and Agamben*. Albany, NY: SUNY Press.

Index